MW00829904

"**Prospect's Bible**" is the first book of the Motorcycle Club Bible series. It is a "how-to" manual that teaches Prospects how to become contributing, lifelong members of law abiding, mighty motorcycle club nations.

$$\underline{B}unch\ \underline{P}ublishing$$

Motorcycle Club Education Division

Copyright © 2014 by

John 'Black Dragon' Edward Bunch II

Library of Congress Control Number: **2014921351**
International Standard Book Number: **978-0-692-34012-7**

i

For information about special discounts for bulk purchases or club purchases please contact Bunch Publishing special sales at 404.692.0336 or bulksales@prospectbible.com.

Black Dragon can speak at your live event. For more information or to book an event contact Bunch Publishing at 404.692.0336 or blackdragon@prospectbible.com

www.bunchpublishing.com
www.prospectsbible.com

Dedication

To: My dearly departed mother, Anese Yvonne Jackson Bunch, who passed away before ever seeing me accomplish anything of significance. For working yourself to the bone so that I might become someone I am forever grateful. I miss you momma. 1942 – 1997

To: My Aunt Bernita Hall, my second mom my entire life!

To: The Buckner's of OKC for four generations of family! Thank you!

To: My grandson, Mandel 'Boogey Man' Jr., you have been left a legacy on two wheels. On your father's side, your dad, grandfather and great grandfather followed the path of Mighty 1%er Outlaw Motorcycle Club Nations. On your mother's side, I have followed the path of a Mighty 99%er law-abiding Motorcycle Club Nation. One day, should you decide to join a MC brotherhood, you will have a choice: to follow the path of the 1%er or the path of the 99%er. Since your lineage is from both sides of the fence your path may seem unclear. My desire is that you will choose the path of peace and not the violent path of the outlaw.

To: Paul 'Pep' Perry, Original Seven, former First Rider and first National President of the Mighty Black Sabbath Motorcycle Club Nation. Thank you for believing in me from Prospect to Technical Advisor on Biker Boyz to grooming me to become First Rider. My goal has been to make you proud and to continue the legacy that the Original Seven established at 4280 Market Street in 1974.

To: 'Super Model' Leigh Forbes, your incredible expectations of me helped push me to match your drive. Thanks for caring for Hope. She is my world as you know.

To: Keith Quinton Corley, in 1995 you spent $2,000 of your bonus money to buy me a laptop for Christmas. You told me to be a writer if that was my dream. Thank you.

To: Attorney Lee Fowler Schwimmer, Counselor, you always pushed me to be greater than I was. Your friendship and guidance, care and concern helped shaped me. Thank you.

To: Bob Schultz, thank you for teaching me how to work on motorcycles. Give a man a fish! I still long for the days when my motorcycle sat on your lift – it was much easier then! ☺

To: Robert Coleman, thank you for the fire-side chats and for lifting weights with me at lunch. Our competitive spirits have pushed me forward to achieve. I still believe I'll get down to 289 pounds before you get to 285. When I do, "I want my QUARTER!!!!!"

To: Christin Chapman, thank you for helping me to get past it. And for working out with me every day for almost a year, until I lost nearly 100 pounds! We said we would do it. We did it.

To: Robert 'Brother Bob' Banks, you took in a wayward, young prospect and taught him to ride Gold Wings, travel cross country through wild thunderstorms and 100 degree days – and to sleep under the stars on the open road like a true Nomad. You took a young man under your wing and groomed him like a son. And you helped create the National President of the Mighty Black Sabbath Motorcycle Club Nation. I am you. Thank you.

Thanks for Supporting Me

To: Tommy 'Hog Man' Lewis, National Vice President of the Mighty Black Sabbath Motorcycle Club Nation. Thank you for believing in me and supporting my vision. Also, Master Chief, thank you for teaching me how to lead a nation.

To: Uncle J.P. Hall. Thank you for being a man of God, honor, family, principle and strength. Your example has always been my inspiration!

Thanks Shirley Knight, she has become an amazing woman of Christ!

To: Huggy Bear, Krow, Chill, Eight Ball, Ride or Die, Big Dale and Hollywood. You Regional Presidents, past and present, have spread our message across the nation! Continue to serve your brothers and sisters with honor, love, pride and distinction.

To: Presidents of the Mighty Black Sabbath Motorcycle Club Nation. Never forget that you are the servants of our people. They follow because they love you. Always deserve that love by never violating their trust.

To: Allen 'Sugar Man' Brooks, High Council Prez. Told you we could!

To the full patched Brothers, Sisters of the Cross, Goddesses, Support Crew, Auxiliary, Prospects and Hang-Arounds of the Mighty Black Sabbath Motorcycle Club Nation, in everything that we do let us always show the world why we are 'A Breed Apart' since 1974 and still strong!

To my sisters, Thea and Lori, and my cousins, Billy, Tony, Be Be, Latrina, Veronica and Keisha, I miss our childhood and summers in Wichita, Kansas. I wish we could go back there and play jacks again.

To my editors Robert Schultz, Christin Chapman and Robert Coleman, thank you for allowing me to appear competent and literate.

To: George 'Magic' Gilbert Clark III. Thank you Master Chief for bringing me to the Mighty Black Sabbath Motorcycle Club Nation!

To: Pappy, By the Book, Coach, Lil' Big Mac, Boaz, OL Skool, Ice Man, G-Baby, Full House, Freight Train, Strictly Business, Marine, G Man, Jerzee, Swerve, Jay Rock, Justice, Wide Track, SAT and Libra, your strength in Atlanta allowed me to re-launch a nation that spread from coast to coast! Though we didn't always get along, I thank you!

To: My Darling Daughter Tanisha, you were there when I was at my lowest moment to mend your daddy's broken heart, thus making you my greatest hero. Did you know that?

A prospect lives to serve the MC

A prospect never fails the MC

A prospect volunteers without having to be asked

A prospect represents his patch with honor

A prospect is proud to prospect and does so with glee

A prospect is always silent unless spoken to

A prospect acknowledges no name other than "Prospect"

A prospect never speaks ill of his full patch brothers

A prospect never discusses MC business with others

A prospect never attempts to speak for the MC

A prospect never lies to his brothers

A prospect doesn't take sides in MC politics

A prospect always protects the President

A prospect always arrives on two wheels regardless of weather

A prospect learns his bylaws

A prospect learns his MC's history

A prospect knows what his colors represent

A prospect is always humble and never starts fights

A prospect never asks when his prospectship will end

"We all reserve the right to get smarter later.

That being said, however, the stupid shall be punished!**"**

Cmdr. Gary E. Williams
Commanding Officer USS Memphis SSN 691
March 28, 1989 – November 11, 1989
Hunter/Killer Fast Attack Submarine

Prospect's Bible
"How to Prospect for a Traditional Law Abiding MC"

By:
John Edward Bunch II
Black Dragon
National President
Mighty Black Sabbath Motorcycle Club Nation
A Breed Apart
Since 1974 and Still Strong..............................///
www.blacksabbathmc.com
www.blacksabbathmagazine.com
blackdragon@prospectbible.com

Love, Honor, Perseverance, Duty, Courage, Loyalty...

Edited by:
- Christin Chapman
- Robert 'Bob' Coleman
- Robert 'Bob' Schultz

First Edition, First Printing November 2014

www.prospectsbible.com

Foreword

When I first joined the Motorcycle Club (MC), I was a gullible, shy kid from Oklahoma City, new to San Diego, having never been away from home and alone in the adult world. I was a young Navy man serving aboard a 688 Los Angeles class Fast Attack Hunter/Killer nuclear Submarine named the USS Salt Lake City SSN 716. I thought the Silent Service had made me tough but when I stumbled upon the MC I was awe-struck and immediately smitten. I saw that patch and the brothers who wore it and I wanted to be just like them, one of them, part of them—no matter what it took.

During that time the MC was the top 99%er MC on the San Diego Black Biker Set, having stood nearly twenty years, with the only clubhouse in San Diego. The brothers were arrogant and they really did not feel like they needed new members. They used to say, "We don't need anybody. We are the top of the food chain!" So they made it nearly impossible for any Prospects to crossover. We was poorly treated, mishandled, bullied and verbally abused. To add to that my prospectship began right in the middle of a civil war. No brother was going to vote in a Prospect who could vote for the opposite side, so I was stuck in the middle.

I was also a lazy Prospect. I had an attitude of entitlement. I wanted to take short cuts instead of working as hard as I could to get the hard stuff over and behind me. I never liked cleaning up the clubhouse or any of the menial tasks so I half-assed everything. The brothers saw this. With all of the politics, coupled with my less than stellar attitude, I was not allowed to crossover for years. My Prospect patch was taken many times and the MC told me over and over that I would never be a full patched brother. Still I would not be denied. So I continued forward even though it took years before I could cross. I was hard riding and mentally committed! Once I made up my mind that I wanted in, nothing and nobody was going to stop me. I was not going to quit! They were going to cross me over into the brotherhood if I had to Prospect for ten years! Unfortunately, it took nearly five.

One day, President Pep recognized me. For some reason he just took an interest in me and began to develop and tutor my hard head. He stood up for me and brushed aside those who were determined to keep me out. Pep became determined that I would succeed, teaching me how to be a contributing part of the MC brotherhood.

When the San Diego City Attorney went after the MC and decided to shut us down, I used the power of my best friend's newspaper to soften up the city by writing article after article about how they were pushing our MC around. It was not a good look for the city so the area police Captain gave me a call and asked for a meeting. I was able to negotiate a meeting between the area police Captain, the City Attorney and the MC. After that meeting we were allowed to keep our doors open and the harassment ended.

Finally, I had become a contributor. My pen went to work and won on behalf of the MC! Pep was proud. Now I deserved to be crossed over into the brotherhood and Pep saw that it was so.

Then Pep taught me to be a leader. Late hot summer nights in the clubhouse Pep would teach. His wife had kicked him out of his house and my girlfriend had kicked me out of mine. So we would sleep on the clubhouse floor where it was cool and look up at the ceiling. He told me about his dreams to have a mighty MC Nation one day. At that time we had only two chapters. He wanted an MC that all would know, that would spread its reach be from sea to shining sea. He told me that Coochie had made Magic promise on his death bed that the MC would always remain intact. Though I never met Coochie, I promised myself that if no others could, I would keep that promise Magic made. I called it "Coouchie's Promise" and I pursue it even to this day. Pep also taught me how to love the MC and to put the brothers and sisters of the MC always before myself. Pep would say, "We, we, we, not me, me, me! Twenty-one years later Pep turned the MC he and six others founded over to me. I became the second First Rider and second National President of the Mighty Black Sabbath Motorcycle Club Nation.

Are You Worthy to Prospect for a Patch?

When you think you have gone as far as you can go with these mean assholes who would one day call themselves your brothers. When the love of your life says "I quit, you are not the one!" and your family thinks you have gone mad for hanging out with those losers. When your friends ask you not to drop by wearing those colors and your daughter tells her preacher that her father is a member of a gang. When the MC is threatened and standing next to your brothers could cost you your very life! When, despite all that you have freely given, the MC has broken every promise it ever made to you, stabbed you in the back and let you down so bad you never want to see any of those #$%@$ again!

Can You Stand!?

Only then will you know if you have what it takes to stand true and tall, a warrior of the Mighty Black Sabbath Motorcycle Club Nation or any other MC Nation to which you would aspire to belong.

If you can't still love your chosen MC after loss, humiliation, defeat, abuse, let-down, struggle, hard work, sadness, frustration, fear, death, war, civil war and disappointment—the MC life is NOT FOR YOU! You will either be a club hopper, groupie or malcontent for the rest of your MC career but you will never be family. Yes, there are great times as well. The greatest of times are when your brotherhood is riding together as one on two!

I am John Edward Bunch II known to the Biker Set as 'Black Dragon'. My experience comes from my twenty-four years as a full patched brother of the Mighty Black Sabbath Motorcycle Club Nation, of which (at the time of this writing) I am the National President. My entire MC career has been spent in this forty-one year old, traditional 99%er, law abiding, MC Nation. I am proudly a 99%er! I made the decision decades ago to live my MC life on this side of the fence. I speak to you from the experiences I have gleaned from this lifestyle. I was not a great Prospect. But you can be!

Table of Contents

Contents

Introduction

Welcome to the incredible world of motorcycle clubs! If you find a group of brothers who unbelievably share the same passion you have for living, riding, being on motorcycles, and sharing their lives with their club brothers, unselfishly, forever—you will be blessed beyond your wildest imagination. Should you decide to become one with them, you will need to prospect to earn their respect and brotherhood. These pages will teach you to do it right! You will learn how to prospect with honor, distinction and pride. It is my greatest pleasure to show you what I've learned over the past twenty-four years as a member of the Mighty Black Sabbath Motorcycle Club Nation. Perhaps you will be able to learn from my mistakes so that you won't repeat them.

Your first lesson is to learn how to love others more than you love yourself. Your entire MC career, if it is to be successful, will hinge upon your ability to put the best interests of the MC above your own. You have to love more than a back patch. You have to love the people represented by that patch. A patch does not make a MC. The people do. The MC is about the people who make up its membership. Love the people and you will love the MC. Love the MC and you will always represent that patch with honor.

Prospects / Probationaries / Probies

If you are interested in what prospecting for a traditional MC is all about keep turning the pages. This book is for those who want to do things the right way; the way their MC's forefathers and MC legends did things. Prospect's Bible will instruct you in what it takes to become a hard core, hot running, results producing Prospect that any traditional MC would want to crossover into full patched brotherhood.

Who Should Read "The Prospect's Bible"

- Anyone considering joining a traditional 99%er law abiding MC.
- Anyone hanging around a MC who wants to know more about how MCs operate.
- Anyone currently prospecting for a MC.
- Anyone who has the responsibility of training or is a sponsor of your MC's Prospects.
- Anyone starting up a new MC.
- Any President or other club officer of an established MC.
- Anyone desiring more education about the beginning steps of learning Biker Set protocol, selecting and gaining membership in a traditional MC or learning the meaning of true prospecting for a traditional 99%er law abiding MC.

1%er Nation Prospects and Hang-Arounds

I don't claim to have any knowledge about the way 1%er nations handle their Prospects and hang-arounds. The inner workings of that world are foreign to me. Where similarities exist to traditional 99%er law abiding MCs, perhaps this book may be of some use to you. Love, honor, loyalty and respect are common values any MC looks for in a Prospect. Think of others before you think of yourself, concern yourself with accomplishing the best interests of the MC at all times and present yourself as an open book containing all of the very best qualities you would expect to receive and you will be fine. Go with God and ride safely. Be Blessed!

Traditional 99%er Law Abiding MC

This book was written to teach you how to have success primarily in prospecting for traditional 99%er law abiding MC nations because that is where my experience in the MC world has been over the past twenty-four years.

You Don't Do Rules, Regulations & Responsibilities

The MC world has existed for nearly one hundred years in America. There are protocols, rules, customs and traditions that are enforced on the MC Biker Set that have been in place long before you showed up on the horizon riding two. This is not the world you want it to be. This is the world that is. You don't have to become involved. You can continue riding FREE with the wind in your face and the bugs in your teeth and no biker in the MC world will even notice your scooter as you putt by. You will remain unmolested and a freestyle independent biker. But should you don a set of colors upon your back understand that you will be expected to play this game by our rules or you won't be allowed to play at all. You won't change this game as many before you have tried and failed. If you can't abide by the stipulations of the MC lifestyle—leave the colors alone. There is no shame in riding as an independent. We will still hang out with you and sometimes let you ride with us.

Why I Wrote the Prospect's Bible

This book was born of my never ending love for the Mighty Black Sabbath Motorcycle Club Nation. It was my desire to help solve the problems of member retention, club hopping, disrespectful behavior and the "ME-first" attitude of members leading to destructive behavior that has tainted the reputation of the Mighty Black Sabbath Motorcycle Club Nation and many other MC nations on Biker Sets across the world.

I wrote this book to teach Prospects their duties and obligations owed to the MC and the concepts of MC Biker Set life from the 99%er prospective. I also wanted to clear up some of the misconceptions that I helped to spread across the Biker Set as Technical Advisor to the DreamWorks© movie, Biker Boyz©. I failed to do an adequate job of portraying the rules of the Biker Set leaving newbies the impression that belonging to the MC culture is more about designing colors on a laptop, slapping them on their backs and "popping up" than it is about knowing the history, protocol, discipline, tradition, and brotherhood of bonding as family for the rest of their lives.

Chapter 1: Motorcycle Clubs

What Kinds of MCs Can I Join

There are many kinds of motorcycle riding organizations to which you can belong. Some, you pay your initiation fees and "presto" you are a member. Others actually require you to Prospect but are only recreational and therefore have no emphasis on a MC family. There are American Motorcyclist Association (AMA) sponsored MCs, Riding Clubs (RCs), Motorsports Clubs (MSC), Car/Bike Clubs, mixed MCs with social clubs (MS/SC), religious riding associations like the Christian Motorcyclist Association (CMA), secular riding associations like the Gold Wing Road Riders Association (GWRRA) and service riding associations like the Patriot Guard. As you can see there are many classifications from which to choose. Motorcycle clubs (MCs) are different from any of the others. Whether 99%er or 1%er, the MC is at the top of the food chain because their level of organization, training, marketing, unity of family, security and dedication is unmatched by any other biker organization. Ultimately all bikers want to belong to a MC but the lifestyle is not for everyone. Though many attempt to join, few are chosen to be brothers of an elite MC. Being a brother is challenging. It is hard work as the MC will take up a lot of your time for the rest of your life! So it is important to consider before joining, if you don't have time, join instead one of those motorsports biking organizations and have a blast riding. It will be recreational only and that is ok.

What is a Motorcycle Club

A motorcycle club (MC) is a group of motorcycle owning/riding individuals who bond together as brothers—agreeing to adhere, for the rest of their lives, to the Biker Set lifestyle, culture, MC protocols, customs and traditions; then ride, live, laugh, love, cry and die together—no longer as individuals but now as ONE extended family, under a code of conduct, known as the bylaws, and a unified flag, known as the colors, worn on a vest, known as a cut. Until death do them part! Amen.

Why Join a Motorcycle Club

Most people who join MCs are looking for something more than they have in their personal lives. They have a need that ordinary folk don't have—to put a symbol on their backs and boast that affiliation to the world. They need to belong to the herd, to be a part of the pack and to run with the squad. Many claim that they make the patch and that the patch does not make them, but if that were so true why wear a patch at all? It is okay to need the pack. That is why folks have created organizations throughout the centuries to which you may belong. There is no need to be ashamed of this need or to fear it. Wanting to belong to a brotherhood bonded by the love of riding the steel is ok. If you desire that brotherhood and extended family you should go for it! You only do yourself a disservice if you don't research, study and discover a MC worthy of being your extended "family." When you do you should exhaust yourself proving that you are worthy of being a "brother" of that MC.

Beware. Not every MC is traditional.

Look-alike Motorcycle Clubs

Often folks will band together in a social context to ride and consider themselves a MC. But for those of us who live the true MC lifestyle, defined by the subculture known as the Biker Set, these folks would be thought of as merely a riding club, social club, mixture club or social experiment. It can be misleading at first when you approach these so called MCs. They look very much like the real thing. Often you don't find out any better until long after you have been a member. Tread cautiously when you are looking for a MC to join because a dedicated biker only wants to choose a MC one time in his life. Choose well.

Why Join a Traditional 99%er Law Abiding MC

If you are choosing a traditional MC there are two ways you can go: a 99%er law abiding MC or 1%er outlaw MC. Both come with their own sets of problems. 99%er MCs concentrate on riding and enjoying their MC families. They refute violence and don't condone MC sponsored illegal activities. They are able to ride anywhere without having to worry about being in the wrong area where they may be attacked or threatened by rival 1%er MCs because they are neutral. The down side is that the 99%er MCs are not dominant so they exist under rules defined by 1%er MCs who control them to some extent, especially as it relates to where they can open chapters and what their colors might look like (a problem for new MCs). That is simply the way it is. Historic 99%er MCs, that have been around for decades, have already resolved these types of issues and these concerns with the 1%er MCs and are respected and allowed to ride freely. They train their Prospects to follow Biker Set protocol and seldom experience problems because they stay in their own lanes. Newer 99%ers and pop-up MCs trying to establish themselves have a tougher time getting up and running.

Traditional 99%er law abiding MCs also follow written bylaws. They Prospect their hang-arounds. They operate a democratic society that abides by the majority vote! You cannot buy a traditional 99%er patch or negotiate your way into the family. You must own a motorcycle, have a motorcycle license, be a certain age, and have a verifiable source of legal income. You must complete a comprehensive prospectship of at least ninety days and win a 100% vote of the members. You must then pledge allegiance to the MC and swear an oath to obey their bylaws, customs and traditions before you may gain entry into their brotherhood.

The traditional 99%er brotherhood is an extended family. It is NOT just a riding club, social club, motorsports club or social experiment. There are some major differences between a traditional 99%er MC and the others, although many modern MCs cross the lines or blur them severely. A traditional MC cannot be mistaken and you will be able to soon see if it is the kind of MC you have approached and are trying to learn:

1. In a traditional 99%er law abiding MC, the order of importance the MC shall play in your life will be as follows:
   a. God
   b. Family
   c. Job
   d. MC

   This may be different from the 1%er MC lifestyle that, I have heard, puts the MC first above all else.

2. In a traditional 99%er law abiding MC, the primary purpose of the MC is to build an extended family upon which you can depend for the rest of your life based around the love and lifestyle of riding motorcycles and spending your free time with those brothers and sisters of the MC who share your passion for the iron and love of the road.

3. A traditional 99%er law abiding MC is an elite motorcycle enthusiast riding organization. You will be expected to ride like nomads not sit around on bar stools in the clubhouse telling tall tales about riding hard.

4. A traditional 99%er law abiding MC gives each Prospect written bylaws. No member is above the MC's bylaws.

5. A traditional 99%er law abiding MC relies on officers to lead. These officers are democratically elected by full patched brothers in good standing during regularly held elections—based on election rules specified in the bylaws.

6. A traditional 99%er law abiding MC uses the democratic vote of full patched brothers in good standing to decide the MC's direction and empowers the officers to lead the MC in the direction in which the brothers have voted.

7. A traditional 99%er law abiding MC will convene a board to handle all disciplinary problems and allow the accused to face his accusers and fight written charges levied against him.

8. A traditional 99%er law abiding MC will hear appeals of members who have lost disciplinary hearings.

9. In a traditional 99%er law abiding MC no officer or member may snatch your colors at a whim or without a board of the committee or charges being filed. There are no kings; situations will be handled fairly.

10. A traditional 99%er law abiding MC rides in the pack in formation two by two (two up abreast) and not staggered unless weather or road conditions dictate).

11. A traditional 99%er law abiding MC will pound across country on two wheels and use a tow or chase vehicle (if at all) for emergencies only—NOT the other way around.
12. A traditional 99%er law abiding MC will never initiate violence, lay claim to or stake territory.
13. A traditional 99%er law abiding MC does not wear a state-only bottom rocker.
14. A traditional 99%er law abiding MC will wear a bottom rocker or one-piece only club back patch that lists a city or city, state.
15. A traditional 99%er law abiding MC does not wear a diamond patch of any kind or the words 1%er or outlaw anywhere on their cut.
16. A traditional 99%er law abiding MC does not engage in nefarious activities or sanction non law-abiding activities of any kind.
17. A traditional 99%er law abiding MC does not engage in prostitution, gun running, drug running, extortion, conspiracy, theft, racketeering or any other organized crime.
18. Members of a traditional 99%er law abiding MC may never physically fight one another. Punch a brother and you are out! We are brothers not hoodlums! You can; however, put on the gloves!
19. A 99%er traditional law abiding MC Prospects all of its members. You will be required to Prospect your way in no matter what your rank or position was in any other MC or organization. There are few exceptions to that rule.
20. In a traditional 99%er law abiding MC you will be given a sponsor to guide you through your prospectship and educate you on MC bylaws, protocol, customs and traditions.
21. In a traditional 99%er law abiding MC Prospects will not be allowed to speak directly in any club meetings, gatherings

or functions. You will instead speak through your MC
sponsor and you will always remain silent while on the Biker
Set.

22. In a traditional 99%er law abiding MC your name will be
Prospect X until you crossover, then the MC names you—
you do not name yourself.

The law abiding MC extended family supports you 100% through
life's greater and lesser moments. Its brothers are commonly
bonded by their love of motorcycles; the culture, protocol and
lifestyle of freedom-loving bikers living on the Biker Set. If you
desire the lifestyle of the traditional 99%er law abiding MC then you
should find one and start prospecting.

How Do I Choose a MC

Hang around! It is probably foolish to join the first MC you come
across without checking out others; still many hang-arounds do that
very thing. I did it! I spent ten minutes in the mother chapter of the
Mighty Black Sabbath Motorcycle Club Nation and I was instantly
hooked. I prospected and twenty-four years later have never looked
back. So you have to go with your instincts and your gut. Sometimes
you will hit that perfect match the first time. Sometimes you may
need to hang around several MCs before you find the right one.
Perhaps the scientific way to choose a MC is to hang around a few,
learn what you can and narrow it down from there. I think if more
people hung around a few MCs before joining one, MCs would have
fewer turnovers. Above all, you must look for a MC that has the
same values, morals, customs and traditions you can identify with
and align yourself to follow.

How Do I Find MCs to Hang Around and Get to Know

The Old Fashioned Way: Go to wherever bikers may hang out. Eventually you will find some guys walking around with patches on their backs. You may find them at a bike rally, sporting event or local pub. If they are not 1%er MCs they will be easy enough to approach. Introduce yourself and let them know that you have an interest in learning about joining a MC. They will take you under their wing and you will be on your way.

The Hi-Tech Way: Get on the internet and start searching. Many people have come to the Mighty Black Sabbath Motorcycle Club Nation after following us on social media, our website (www.blacksabbathmc.com), our phone apps ("Black Sabbath Motorcycle Club") and our online magazine (www.blacksabbathmagazine.com). Then send an email to the contact person listed, stating your interest. You will find what you are looking for.

How Do I Gain Entry into a MC

Entry into a MC depends upon the MC. Some MCs allow you to pay for a patch and as soon as you put the money on the table you are given your colors and you instantly become a member. These are not "traditional" MCs. In this book I focus on traditional 99%er law abiding MCs. If you want to become a member of a traditional 99%er MC you will have to become a hang-around, then become a

Prospect, completing prospectship before gaining entry. This prospectship is also known as prospecting, being a probie, serving a prospectship or serving probation.

What is A Hang-Around

"Hang-around" is the official name for a person who is trying to get to know a MC for the purposes of becoming a Prospect. You can spend time with a MC and hang out at the clubhouse every night and not be considered a hang-around. When you become a hang-around, the MC has formally acknowledged that you are at a stage where you want to learn more about the MC for the purposes of prospecting for that MC. Some MCs will vote you in as a hang-around. Some MCs will have a set of requirements that you will have to complete before you can transition from being a hang-around to being voted in as Prospect. For instance, you might have to complete two official runs with the MC and attend two club meetings before you can ask for a vote to become a Prospect. These requirements may take months to complete. As a hang-around you can expect to be treated like a Prospect during that time because the MC will be assigning you tasks and treating you like a Prospect in many cases. Act like a Prospect and conduct yourself with honor and soon you will be a Prospect.

What is a Prospectship

"Prospectship" is the period of time a Prospect serves the MC after which he will be required to receive a 100% up vote to become a member. In a traditional MC if even one member objects to a Prospect's crossing over to become a member, the Prospect cannot become a member. This may not be the end for a Prospect. Sometimes a Prospect can be assigned extra time so that he can fix his deficiencies and eventually earn the 100% up vote of his prospective brothers. To be successful think of the prospectship as a probationary time you get to prove to the MC that you are worthy of becoming a full patched brother of the MC and the newest member of the MC family. It is also important to remember that the prospectship is a two-way journey. This is also the time when the MC proves to you that it is worthy of your loyalty, time and consideration. If during the prospectship, there is a time that either the MC or the Prospect loses confidence in the other the prospectship can be severed with no hard feelings.

What is a Prospect

"Prospect", "Probie", "Probationary" or "P" all refer to the official position of a person who has been voted in by the full patched brothers to begin his prospectship. Whether you are called Prospect or Probie will be determined by the area of the country in which your MC is located, or the history of that MC. For instance, many East Coast MCs call their initiating brothers Probies, yet when those MCs open chapters on the West Coast they wouldn't start calling them Prospects, as most West Coast MCs do. Often they may still call these prospective members Probies as is the MC's tradition. No matter what you are called, Prospect, Probie, Probationary or simply "P", Prospect is the first level of membership any person may attain in a traditional 99%er law abiding MC.

What is the Purpose of the Prospectship

The purpose of the prospectship is for the Prospect to get to know the MC and for the MC to get to know and trust the Prospect as a brother in the MC. The prospectship may be difficult as members will devise interesting and uncomfortable ways to get under the Prospect's skin. Asking Prospects to clean the clubhouse, take out the trash, accomplish unpleasant tasks, run errands and/or wash motorcycles are normal requests. The prospectship is designed to be difficult to bring out the true character of the Prospect and allow the Prospect, as well as the MC, to decide if they like each other enough to be family—but overall it should be a fun, unique and rewarding experience. Remember Prospects are the MC's future. If they are all driven away the MC will die an untimely death. It is in the MC's best interest to have successful prospecting programs that generate quality members.

The Art of Prospecting

Prospecting is the act of learning the history, traditions, values and core beliefs of a MC while proving your worthiness for brotherhood through service, patience and humility. The Prospect should view the prospectship as a time of honorable service and should use the time to both evaluate the MC's culture as well as demonstrate his ability to be a good fit for the MC. A successful Prospect should seek to learn all there is to know about the MC's daily functions, charitable contributions, member personalities, MC riding style and the MC's allies and enemies. If a Prospect is unclear about any aspect of the MC after the prospectship is over then the Prospect has failed himself and the MC.

The Goal of a Prospect
This should be repeated daily...
"To find a worthy MC and earn the right to join its brotherhood and become a part of that extended MC riding family to which I can belong for the rest of my life. Then engage myself in the day-to-day business of serving my MC family forever."

I Want In, I Just Don't Want to Prospect
If the MC that interests you is worth being included in your extended family then it is worth prospecting for, so that you might earn your way into the brotherhood. There are many excuses I hear people use to explain why they should not have to Prospect:

- I am a "masonic buffalo" brother-of-the-horn why should I Prospect for your MC? I've already done this in an organization way bigger than your little MC!
- I am a grown man I am not prospecting for anyone and taking that BS, I am far too mature for anyone to throw water on me so why should a grown man Prospect for your MC?
- I just don't feel like taking that prospecting crap off of anybody.
- If your MC can't take me like I am and just trust me enough to give me a patch then to heck with them because I can't be in a MC that does not trust me.
- I am a multi-millionaire professional football player for the NFL on an award winning team, no one in that MC makes near enough money to Prospect me! With all of my money, fortune and fame I bring more to your MC than it brings to me so why should I Prospect? You should be happy to have me because just having me will bring new members to your MC!

- A Prospect is a nobody and I just can't be a nobody for any length of time—not even for a second, for anybody, I don't care who your MC is.
- They are not going to haze me!
- I was a Sgt-at-Arms in my last MC and a President in my last MC before that, and I was the VP of the MC I was in before that one and I have been hanging out in your MC for so long that everyone knows me. Why should I have to Prospect all over again?
- My father was the founder of this MC and I am a member by blood right! I shouldn't have to Prospect!

You Prospect for the MC to earn your way into the brotherhood. During your prospectship the MC exposes you to its culture, history, bylaws and traditions so that you can know that the MC is worthy of your membership. This is a priceless relationship and a process that must occur if you intend on being a member for life. And that is what a traditional MC wants—members for life. If your fraternal organization is so great, then put their MC patch on your back and ride with them. After all, you did pledge for them and many fraternal organizations are converting their symbols to back patches and riding under MC bylaws these days. But if you desire the brotherhood of a traditional MC you shouldn't mind working hard to earn it. There is no aristocracy in a traditional law-abiding MC. There are no blood lines to membership or leadership. In a traditional MC members are voted in, officers are voted up and decisions are voted on before they become law. A brother is not guaranteed entry into the MC just because his grandfather was the founder of that MC, nor is he guaranteed to become an officer or the President of that MC because his father was a President. Either you earn your way in or carry yourself on to one of those non-traditional MCs that give away or sell patches. A traditional MC looks for lifetime members by treating everyone fairly as promised in its bylaws. Carry your weight and earn your way in. You will be damned proud that you did!

How do I become a Prospect?

You will spend an amount of time as a hang-around and complete the necessary steps to become eligible to be a Prospect. Once you are eligible, the MC will hold a vote. If 100% of the full patched brothers vote in the affirmative you will be sworn in as a Prospect. A Prospect must swear into the MC just like a member. This will be one of three times you will swear into the MC. The second time will be when you become a full patched member and the third time is when you become an officer. During the swearing in ceremony you may have to answer questions about why you want to be a member of the MC or why you think the MC is for you.

1. It is always best to answer these questions with what you think you can bring to the MC more than what you think you can get from the MC.
2. Demonstrate that you've done some homework as a hang-around and be prepared to answer questions about the history, traditions and customs of your prospective MC. (Everyone likes a hot runner who knows a thing or two about the MC they want to join.)
3. Be humble and sincere, but also be a man. Everyone appreciates a prospective brother who is going to call things like they see them, with confidence—not cockiness. Everyone hates arrogant people, especially if they have no reason to be arrogant—especially if you haven't earned your way in yet.

4. Approach answering your questions from the perspective of being a servant to the MC. Get used to serving the MC, because you will be doing so for the rest of your life.

Upon successful completion of the swearing in ceremony you will lose your name and identity to the MC. You will become a member with no name other than that of "Prospect" and your Prospect number. For instance your name could be "Prospect X" of the Atlanta, GA chapter.

Bylaws

After you become "Prospect X" you will be given a set of bylaws. This may be the first time you have ever heard of the bylaws. The bylaws will be the most important document the MC will ever give you. That is because the bylaws are your contract with the MC and they are the promise from the MC that if you conduct yourself according to the bylaws you will forever be a full patched brother within the mighty MC Nation you have chosen to join and no one or nothing can change that. The bylaws are the detailed instructions that set out the constitution and the day-to-day governance of your MC. The bylaws are the glue by which the members of the entire MC family are adhered together. You will learn these bylaws over the course of your prospectship. If you fail to know those bylaws nearly word for word after your prospectship is completed you will have failed yourself and your MC.

Club Sponsor

A club sponsor will also be assigned to you when you swear in and become a Prospect. The club sponsor should be a senior member with enough clout to educate and protect you from unruly or untoward members during your prospectship. Your sponsor may actually be a member who recruited you or someone else who is so designated with the task of bringing you up to speed. In any event, your club sponsor is your lifeline and your bridge into the MC. Keep him close and stay in constant contact with him. In traditional MCs you won't be able to speak in club meetings or in any public place. You will communicate through your sponsor so every aspect of your early MC life will be his concern. Keep him in the loop. Ask him thousands of questions. Write down what he tells you to do and then do it, research it or learn it. Make yourself this man's shadow. Learn all you can from him. Your club sponsor is your crowned jewel. Use his knowledge to propel yourself forward.

If you have a bad sponsor find someone else willing to teach you the ways of the MC and latch onto them instead! Absorb anything they are willing to teach you.

Modern MCs and Prospecting

Modern MCs often mistake the prospectship as a time to play college-like fraternity games that include unacceptable forms of hazing, public displays of humiliation, sexual harassment (clubs who take in female members), coercion, and physical brutality imposed upon Prospects. This is an aspect of immaturity that many modern MCs are currently experiencing. Other modern MCs have not made the determination as to whether they want to be outlaws or law-abiding MCs and have prospectships that include asking Prospects to participate in illegal activities, fighting, assaults and all sorts of other madness. I have seen still other modern MCs line all of their Prospects up at MC annuals, then go around and gather other MC's prospects and haze them all in a group—forcing Prospects to stand on one leg, chant silly slogans, stand up holding signs above their arms until they can no longer lift them —the list goes from the silly to the absurd. I am often confounded to see thirty and forty year old or older adults enduring this balderdash while trying to gain entry into a 99%er MC. Why? What should a 99%er MC be doing other than training hard-riding Prospects to become hard-riding members? A 1%er MC may need some kind of wild proof of loyalty but a traditional 99%er law-abiding MC only needs to know that you will ride your bike and be there if times get tough. Beware of these so called "MCs" when you begin prospecting, especially for brand new MCs. Many of them still have a lot to learn.

An Example of Prospecting for a Traditional 99%er MC

Prospects of a traditional MC can expect:

- Prospects are members under probation because they wear the MC's patch, are accountable to the bylaws, pay dues and receive indoctrination. After they complete their prospecting period they become full patched brothers.
- Prospects will never be required to do anything that is demeaning or insulting to their humanity, family-name, racial origin or religion.
- Prospects only Prospect for their MC Nation and NO OTHERS.

- Prospects will never be illegally-hazed, physically abused or sexually harassed.
- Prospects will never be asked to break any laws, participate in physical altercations with any person or risk their lives or freedom to gain membership.

Prospect Rules of Conduct

- A Prospect will always be **SILENT** during all church meetings and public outings with the MC.
- A Prospect will direct all comments, questions or observations through either his sponsor or a regular member (in the absence of his sponsor).
- A Prospect is required to accomplish whatever tasks a full patched member requests of him, but in a 99%er law abiding MC, will be required to do nothing illegal, discrediting or shameful.
- A Prospect will have no name other than Prospect and his Prospect number during the prospectship.
- A Prospect will wear his colors at all times where it would be appropriate for a regular member to wear theirs.
- A Prospect will never pack a woman on his bike while attending any event with the MC. His backseat is reserved for MC use and therefore should not be occupied.
- A Prospect will never interrupt the President when he is speaking or in a conversation with someone.
- A Prospect will never disrespect an officer of another MC.
- A Prospect will never lay his colors on the ground, lose track of them or give them to any person outside of the MC to hold for any reason.

- A Prospect will always make sure his patches are sewn on tightly so no one can snatch them from his vest.
- A Prospect will not chase women while on the Bike Set; he will instead serve the MC.
- A Prospect never cyber bangs! Negative activity of on social media of any kind is strictly forbidden.
- A Prospect will never disclose MC business on social media.

Is a Prospect a Member of the MC

Though a Prospect is not considered a full patched brother, a Prospect is a probationary member of the MC at the most basic level. But just because you are not a full patched brother does not mean you are not a member and you must conduct yourself every day as though you are a full patched member. Here are four reasons why you should consider yourself a member of your prospective MC from the second you sew on your Prospect patch:

1. A hang-around must be voted into a traditional MC (normally 100% in the affirmative) as a Prospect. By the very fact that you are voted into the MC as a Prospect demonstrates that you have been voted into membership. Your position as a Prospect is important and vital to the survival of the MC. You should act accordingly, at all times— like a member!
2. A Prospect is subject to the rights and consequences of the MC's bylaws. In traditional MC's bylaws the rights and responsibilities of Prospects are specifically listed. As a Prospect you can be fined, sanctioned and can have time

added to your prospectship if you violate the bylaws. Unlike hang-arounds, to which the bylaws do not apply, the fact that the MC's bylaws apply to you implies you are a basic member of the MC.

3.   In many traditional MCs, Prospects pay dues. Paying dues is a huge sign that you are a member!

4.   As a Prospect you will serve the MC. You will put in copious amounts of hard work to better the MC. You may wash full patched brother's bikes, provide security protection for the President or Regional President, clean the clubhouse over and over and over again, paint, repair, fix and improve the clubhouse over and over and over again, stand outside in the rain and guard the full patched brothers' motorcycles on a run. You may sleep in the hotel parking lot on the cement guarding the MC's bikes while the full patched brothers are in the hotel rooms sleeping in the air conditioning. You may use your bike to ride back and forth to the store to pick up stuff the full patched brothers are too lazy to get on their own. Look at this work positively and consider it an investment into your MC's future. Complete this work with great pride and enthusiasm. Anything you invest into is something you own. As a part owner of your MC, you should definitely know that you are a member!

Chapter 2
What to look for What to Avoid...

How Does a Traditional MC Operate

A traditional MC operates by observing the bylaws and following the MC vote. This is a simple model. Officers of the MC serve the members and do not hold themselves out as lords over their flock. They are compelled to service by their love of the MC. The President is the ultimate servant of the MC. His job is to deliver to the MC what the MC has requested by way of vote. If the MC votes for something, the President uses his power to make sure the MC's desires happen. When scouting for a MC make sure this simple model is followed. Most traditional MCs will be easy to recognize because they follow this model.

Democratic Society

Look for a democratic process in the MC with one vote per member. A democratic process is the key to happiness and longevity within a MC.

Violations to Club Bylaws

Find out how violations to the MC's bylaws are handled. Discover how will you be treated and what are your rights if charged with a violation of the bylaws.

Case Study 1: Judge, Jury and Executioner

I personally witnessed an angry President walk up to a member he accused of committing a violation and he demanded the member's colors on the spot. The member surrendered his colors and the President then shouted that the member was on suspension, fined him and told him not to contact the MC for sixty days.

The President made the charge—thus making him the prosecutor, carried out the trial—making him the judge, wherein the member was found guilty—making him the jury, and meted out the fine as well as the sentence—making him the executioner. This was all handled on the spot, in front of non-MC members. The full patched brother did not get a chance to challenge any evidence against him, challenge witnesses, hear the charge of the bylaw he broke, call any witness who may have proved him innocent or anything else a reasonable person would consider fair due process, regardless of the organization to which he belonged.

Ask questions to your sponsor about the charging and punishment procedures within the MC. If your President believes himself to be a dictator who can snatch colors at will—you might want to think twice before crossing over to that MC. Knowing what you face before you get there can prepare you.

What to Expect from MC Life

The traditional MC is comprised of individuals who have agreed to come together as family. This extended family offers you the opportunity to become a member of the family after you have successfully completed your prospectship and won a 100% affirmative vote from the brothers. Your MC life will find you including your extended MC family in many things you enjoy in your personal life. After a while you may find that most of your friends, if not all of them, will be comprised of your MC family.

Often I hear lone bikers talk about not joining MCs because of not wanting to obey rules, not wanting to work at understanding protocol, not wanting to go on mandatory rides and not wanting to deal with MC politics involved with being in the MC. They are doing the right thing by not seeking membership. And I have consequently stopped asking people who voice those kinds of opinions to join my MC. They make lousy Prospects and even worse members. The MC way of life is based upon individuals who gather together as family to support, uplift and be a contributing part of the future of the MC. If you are not prepared to make the MC a central part of your life then you should leave the idea of membership alone. Membership is not intended to be a hobby; it is intended to be a way of life. A member who treats the MC like a hobby seldom puts forth an effort that matches that of his brothers and quickly loses the respect and support of the MC. A Prospect that can't make the MC a central component of his life will not be successful in attaining membership into the traditional MC. If you don't have a lot of time to dedicate then you should wait until you do before wasting your time and more importantly the MC's time in an unsuccessful bid at prospecting. You may be able to get into those other MCs as a hobbyist but you won't get into a traditional MC.

Best Interests of the MC Mentality

The MC mindset you should understand from the very beginning simply put is, "What is best for the club comes first!" If you are not able to give your all to the MC with the MC's best interest as a priority, then not only will you be a poor Prospect but you will also be an even sorrier member. There are many ways the MC will disappoint you throughout your prospectship and even throughout your MC career. The MC is made up of humans who make human mistakes. You will be angry, you will be disappointed; you may feel or experience disloyalty, as if you have been abandoned. You may feel like you are the only person working hard and notice that there are seldom helpers. There may even have points in your MC career where you actually HATE the MC. Not every situation you experience within the MC will be positive. How can any situation made up of humans be 100% positive? So, what is it that you will do about it!? For many Prospects the answer is to QUIT! Just as soon as things don't go as planned or as promised, Prospects there for self and not for the best interests of the MC will cry, pout, quit and go home. If they manage to hang out long enough to crossover, they become members that will try to figure out ways to destroy or split up the MC. That kind of member will leave the MC if they lose a vote for office or find some other gripe or complaint upon which to hang their hat. If you can't accept that in life there are disappointments then you will be totally unprepared for the disappointments you will encounter in your life with the MC. Do yourself a favor; don't Prospect for the MC! If you have to quit when you get upset because things don't go your way, then leave the MC alone. If your answer to a situation you can't control is to split up a MC, go behind members' backs, start side-bar conversations and create some kind of coup d'état—you are not interested in what is best for the MC, you are only interested in having your way. If that is the case you are not good for the MC. In fact you are the worst nightmare of the MC and indeed an enemy. The MC will rue the day it ever saw you coming.

What does a *"best interest of the MC mentality"* truly mean? It means that you suck up your disappointments like a man and continue to seek compromise and success in helping the MC become all that it can be. It means that you will allow no harm to come to the MC, no matter what. It means that even if you have to drop your colors that you would rather step down than stand against the MC. Not every brother will have a *"best interest of the MC mentality"*. It is a rare quality that shows up in some leaders and other givers that is often mistaken for weakness. Strive to be the Prospect that puts the best interests of the MC first no matter what and you will never leave the MC.

To Whom Does Your MC Belong

The MC should be owned by the MC members, like a corporation or nonprofit. However, this is not the case for all MCs. Learn early, before you get too much time invested, exactly who owns the MC, the copyrights to the logos and icons, the patches, clubhouse, etc. Your MC may be owned by a single person. This scenario often happens in newly formed and 'pop-up' MCs that are less than ten years old, as many of the 'founders' who are entering the MC world are more interested in running a MC 'business' than forming a MC extended family. They want to exercise extreme control over every aspect of the MC **'they'** founded and want to have a fail-safe button by which they can hold the entire MC hostage when they can't get their way. Don't be afraid to ask, "Who owns this MC?" Is the clubhouse in a single person's name that can change the locks and put the members in the street? Knowing crucial information about the organization you want to join can help you determine if it is the MC for you.

Case Study 2: Who Owns Your MC?

I witnessed a MC wherein the members became dissatisfied with the Founder/President and wanted to replace him. When they tossed him out as President, he got mad and shut down the MC because he owned the copyright. The members had to give up their colors or face law suits for infringing upon **'his'** copyright. He made it simple; it was his way or the highway.

Case Study 3: Who Owns Your MC?

In another instance, I witnessed an ousted Founder/President who, because he owned the colors, started another MC with the same name as the first with a roman numeral II behind it. The former MC could not protest this new MC with their name because the founder owned the copyright to both MCs!

Greedy founders care nothing about respecting time honored MC protocol. The MC is shared by all. It should be no one's personal property. The case studies I mentioned are not a new phenomenon. This absurdity has been going on for decades. In 1970s San Diego there was a club named after a reptile. Then there was a breakaway club from that MC with the same reptile name only with the word "New" in front of it. Though I am much too young to know exactly what happened in that situation I think everyone can agree that this type of behavior is counter-productive. You never see this level of disrespect happen in 1%er nations. There would simply be an extensive blood bath to follow. 99%er MCs could learn a lot about respect from the 1%er nations. Never knowingly participate in such behavior. Leave the MC intact—if you don't like what's going on, start your own MC or join another.

Case Study 4 Know Who the History of your Patch:

After a horrible club rift that stripped him of his presidency, a break-away President of the Black Sabbath Motorcycle Club took the MC's colors and started a new MC, with only a slight variation to our colors. Instead of keeping the MC whole and working from the inside to reclaim what was his position, his reaction was to destroy the unity of the MC and break away. As a result Prospects that entered his new MC without investigating how their colors originated, were forced to face the question of, "Are you part of the real Black Sabbath Motorcycle Club or that other club who took their colors?" This is not the first time an angry, former member has done all in his power to destroy what he once would die to uphold. But the court of the Biker Set opinion is powerful. MC coalitions across the country are beginning to reject this kind of behavior stopping breakaway MCs before they even get started—and asking them to leave their functions.

Be diligent about finding out the true history of your MC colors. Ask where the colors originated. Ask if the MC is a breakaway from a mother chapter with whom they quarreled. Ask if there is an ongoing war that you will be dropped into the middle of the second you put their Prospect patch on your back. Know everything about the colors you are going to wear. Know what every symbol means, every color and every stitch. Don't be the Prospect that becomes a full patched brother then attends another MC party only to be asked to leave because your colors are considered illegitimate on The Set. Don't believe in an organization and commit yourself to it only to find out they are lying about the very symbol on your back. If your prospective MC brothers cannot explain to you every detail about the history of every stitch, color, icon and symbol in that patch, then they probably don't hold it legitimately.

Case Study 5: Ensure that Your Colors are Legitimate

I witnessed a MC attend a big biker party where a local 1%er walked up to them and stripped each member and all of their Prospects of their colors. The problem was that the popup MC did not have a blessing to operate in that area. The dominant was not screwing around and the popup MC quickly learned that. They left the function embarrassed and without their colors. Is this legal? Bottom line is, it can happen legally or illegally.

There are rules to this lifestyle that existed long before you rode in on two. If you are prospecting for a new or popup MC or even an established or historic MC launching chapters in new territories; if they are 99%ers protocol demands that they obtain a blessing from a local or national dominant to enter new areas. Make sure that you ask about their status with the 1%er MCs in their area of operation as you get closer to becoming a Prospect. A good question to ask is if the MC has received its blessings from the local area or national dominant 1%er MC, Know what you are dealing with before you put that Prospect patch on your back. Your life could depend upon it.

If you desire to belong to a traditional 99%er law abiding MC that follows MC Set protocol and does things the right way, investigate the ownership of that MC. If you are involved in a MC where an individual believes they exclusively own the blood, sweat, tears, work-ethic, pride, reputation, strength and unity of an entire MC family and should control their patch like it is his own—I would suggest that you RUN FROM THAT MC! Otherwise, you may live to regret it. Investigate how your colors originated. Make sure they were not stolen from another MC before you put them on your back. If not, you may be entering into a decades-long civil war that has absolutely nothing to do with you—yet places your life on the line. Ensure that MC that you are interested in has been blessed by the local or national 1%er MC to operate in their area.

Trademarks™ and Copyrights®

Before joining a MC you should know that if you ever depart you will have to give back everything. This is simple protocol and in some MCs you swear before you gain membership that all MC emblems, patches, flags and insignia are the property of the MC. Ex-members will return all items when departing the MC. Of this there can be no compromise. The MC has the right to demand all materials back including T-shirts, cup holders, baseball caps, scarves, arm bands, pins and anything else that bears the MC's emblems (even the tattoos on an ex-member's arm must be tattooed over or burned off). Know this going in. It does not matter if you paid for your coats, patches, glasses, hats, goggles, rings or anything else with the MC's logo, you must return these items the day you leave the MC unless the MC formally allows you to keep something. You will not be paid back for those items. This is core tenant and agreement you make with the MC before you accept their colors and buy items with their logos affixed. You can get yourself hurt, seriously injured or even killed if you try to keep MC items should you depart the MC. Even traditional 99%er law abiding MCs won't be screwing around when it comes to their colors. Any MC will do all in its power to preserve the sanctity of their emblems. This may include things that are not so law abiding to protect these colors. Understand the culture behind this lifestyle you are curious about joining so that you can give it all of the respect it demands. If you drop your prospectship or your membership for any reason or are asked to leave, hand those colors back immediately!

Follow the Money!

As a Prospect you won't have any say in the MC's finances. But you should know how your bylaws say finances will be handled. Make sure you see those procedures happening in the club meetings you are allowed to attend. Your responsibility is just to observe. If you don't see things happening as they should, then look for a plausible reason along with a time table as to when things are going to be restored to normal. If these things don't manifest themselves properly you may have a clue as to how MC business situations are handled in that MC.

Case Study 6: Follow the Money

My early years in the MC were spent in a fog. I was so darned happy just to be a member I simply did not pay attention to anything going on around me, especially when it came to the MC's financial business. I worked at the front door, behind the bar, at the annuals, in the parking lot, security, clean up, trash detail and all the while I watched tens of thousands of dollars flow right past me never once questioning where the money was going. When members, who were barely employed, showed up with brand new cars it never dawned on me that the money may have come from the MC's coffers. And since I never knew how much money was in the MC's coffers, I could not have known for sure if our money had been stolen. My MC's bylaws were well published and an accounting of the money was supposed to happen in every club meeting, but there was a time, for a long time, this was simply not happening. When some of the members got angry and demanded an accounting of the books they were called troublemakers and in one instance a member was physically removed from the club meeting. So, I just never questioned where the money went and truly was such a big kid and having fun, it never dawned on me to even want to know.

Later, as I started to find myself in leadership positions I was absolutely astonished to discover just how much of the MC's precious resources had been squandered over the years. Even worse, I began to discover how much was misappropriated, missing and just plain stolen. If I had it to do all over again, I would have been on top of the money as it was my right and duty to do so as a member long before I became an officer. I would have started my observations as a Prospect.

Club Hazing

A traditional 99%er law abiding MC will be more concerned with creating quality members with its prospecting process, rather than shaming, unacceptably hazing or unduly embarrassing prospective members. Check the bylaws for policies regarding the treatment of Prospects. If you can't find any, inquire so that you can make sure the MC's idea of hazing is not going to be more than you can accept.

When it comes to hazing during your prospectship remember that the basic tenant of the Biker Set is RESPECT. Men respect men and any time you or your MC is disrespected on the Biker Set there will always be an issue. It does not matter if the person bringing that disrespect is a prospective brother prospecting you into his MC. If a prospective brother brings disrespect then he has violated MC protocol and a reckoning must occur. We can always remain at peace as long as I respect you and you respect me. Anything other than that will require a course of action necessary to gain respect or have respect acknowledged where it may not have been before. We are a MC not a college fraternity. Men don't "take wood" or allow ourselves to be humiliated so that someone's ego can be stoked. If a man puts his hands on me, I feel disrespected and there will be consequences. If a man speaks to me in a manner that is inappropriate, he has disrespected me. In order to be always respected on the Biker Set never forget—no matter who it is or what the reason; you are a man first, Always hold yourself as such.

Case Study 7: Hazing With a Purpose

My toughest hazing day as a Prospect was when I was asked to ride from San Diego to Tijuana, Mexico to bring back some authentic tacos to the clubhouse. It was only a twenty minute ride into

Mexico from downtown San Diego because you could travel straight across the Mexican border into Mexico without waiting. But coming back could take two to six hours getting through customs. Two and a half hours later I showed up at the clubhouse tacos in hand. I was beaming with pride but my prospective MC brother was not happy and sent me back to Mexico after eating his tacos claiming the tacos were cold. I rode down and bought more tacos and two hours later I stopped a block before the clubhouse and warmed up the tacos in a store's microwave. I showed up at the clubhouse with piping hot tacos. The prospective MC brother was still not satisfied because he claimed that I could not prove that I had been to Mexico because I had no receipt. So back to Mexico I rode. Three hours later I came back with hot tacos and a receipt. Finally my task was finished. I had spent all day riding back and forth fetching tacos but my spirit was high because I had finally accomplished my prospective brother's task. I learned from that lesson to always produce a receipt when on MC business. I have never forgotten that lesson.

Case Study 8: Preoccupation of a Riding MC

For the most part my prospecting time was spent making things happen for the MC. I was cleaning or sweeping, running errands or representing the MC on runs. The full patched brothers spent time taking me on the road to teach me various aspects of riding in the pack. They escorted me from MC to MC introducing me to all of the important people, Presidents, VIPs, and key players I would need to know when I was traveling on the Biker Set alone. They made sure that I was introduced to MCs in San Diego, Los Angeles, San Bernardino, Fresno, Bakersfield, San Francisco, Phoenix, Las Vegas and Oakland. The full patched brothers took me to the East Bay Dragons MC and to all of the Chosen Few MC clubhouses in

California. Their desire was to make sure I was accepted and known in all of the places the Black Sabbath Motorcycle Club hung out. Wearing the patch was not enough for them. They wanted me to be knowledgeable about the Biker Set and MC protocol. They showed me where the Outlaw MC clubhouses were and taught me the protocol when interacting with outlaws. The first ride I ever had with the MC two full patched brothers named Baker (now of the Soul Brothers Motorcycle Club Nation) and DJ (now of the Chosen Few Motorcycle Club Nation) took me to Los Angeles for the weekend. They wrapped me in arms of protection and taught me everything from never parking my motorcycle pointing toward the clubhouse to never taking off my helmet and putting it on the bar. During my prospectship I was trained to be a biker of the Mighty Black Sabbath Motorcycle Club Nation, a Brother of the Cross and a member of the family. At no time was I hit, paddled, pushed, threatened, made to do push-ups, disrespected or set upon. If the preoccupation of a traditional 99%er law abiding MC is not that of teaching a Prospect the riding culture of the Biker Set and preparing a Prospect to understand the new lifestyle then, pray tell, what on Earth is the purpose?

In many new modern and popup MCs of the younger generation you may find a lot of immaturity in hazing. After all, the Black Sabbath mother chapter in San Diego, CA was sixteen years old with a decade and a half of experience prospecting members by the time I prospected. Newer MCs without that experience often take the path of treating Prospects like line brothers pledging a fraternity rather than that of a MC training the next generation of MC leaders. You may experience all types of absurdity from these inexperienced brothers, many of whom never prospected for a MC themselves, as they are the "original" members of a brand new MC and therefore were not "required" to Prospect. It may be a wise idea to find out if you are to be prospected by a newly formed MC of full patched brothers who did not have to Prospect to gain membership. There is nothing worse than being hazed by a person who never had to go through the humiliation they are putting down. Take the time to get an understanding of what to expect. It can save you a lot of time and trouble.

Some MCs hazing practices are just ridiculous and it is up to you whether or not you want to engage in such antics. Once I witnessed a Prospect standing in a clubhouse holding a sign high in the air over his head for nearly two hours. His full patched brother sat there sipping on a beer while this Prospect was trying his best to hoist this sign over his head and not pass out from standing in one place for so long, in another MC's clubhouse, in front of everyone. None of my full patched brothers allowed me to make a public spectacle of myself as they thought such an action would bring shame upon the Mighty Black Sabbath Motorcycle Club Nation. I wondered how holding up that sign might improve the Prospect's riding skills. When comparing my ride back and forth to Mexico for an entire day to this Prospect holding a sign, I wondered if the two hazing episodes had anything in common. Nope! I was not humiliated in public and made to look like a fool in front of others to gain membership into an organization that publically disrespected me.

Don't Get Hazed By Other MCs

You are prospecting for your MC only and no others. Some MCs won't allow you to go anywhere without a full patched brother because they don't want you to run into trouble with idiots who may want to take advantage of your Prospect status but there are some cases where you might be alone and you must always remember that the only MC for which you Prospect is your own.

Case Study 9: Allow No Other MC to Haze You!

I was sitting in a clubhouse when a full patched brother of that MC walked through the packed clubhouse gathering up all of the Prospects (from his MC as well as all of the visiting MCs). The next thing I know he had them all standing up against a wall hopping on one foot! Prospects of other MCs, social clubs and coed clubs, men and women, were all standing against the wall hopping on one foot. Before he got a chance to get anywhere near my Prospects I said to them, "You Prospect for the Mighty Black Sabbath Motorcycle Club Nation alone. Allow no man to ever disrespect you. Make him pay dearly should he try!"

It could be easy for you to fall for such nonsense especially if you are prospecting for a new MC and your brothers don't know any better themselves. Or, if you are out alone and someone wants to inflate their ego by challenging you or attempting to execute some MC crap against you by attempting to haze you in public—like you belong to their MC. Don't fall for such shenanigans. You don't have to answer a barrage of questions, justify your existence, name the lineage of your MC or explain yourself in any manner to anyone on the Biker Set who is not your brother. Always remember that your patch is a membership patch of the MC Nation for which you are prospecting. That patch is due the respect your MC has established on the Biker Set. Educate a fool to recognize, heed and understand:

"Don't make the mistake of disrespecting me or the colors of my Motorcycle Club Nation. I am Prospect X of the XX MC. I am not your Prospect. Now stand aside and allow me to pass!"

Case Study 10: Stand Up For Yourself Always

There was an incident in the late 80's in which Black Sabbath Motorcycle Club Prospect whooped a Black Sabbath President. The Prez made a tactical error and bunched the Prospect up in a corner putting his hands on him, shoving him and disrespecting him behind the bar—because he thought he was a lowly Prospect. That day cost that Black Sabbath Motorcycle Club President an ass whooping and cost the Prospect nearly a year long addition to his prospectship! It was costly, but the Prospect reminded the Black Sabbath Prez that day that no one disrespects a man.

Chapter 3
Successful Prospecting

Prospect's Job description

The job description of a Prospect can be summed up by the following list:

A. Serve the MC as best you can, every single day for as long as your prospectship should last.

B. Learn everything you can about the MC. The history of the MC, its purpose, its mission, its allies and its enemies. By the end of your prospectship if you are not a qualified and respected MC historian, you have failed.

C. Learn everything you can about every member of your local chapter. If they are to be your brothers you will want to know who they are. Take particular interest in the members who are most distant or may not like you as they will also be your brothers. You will need their votes to gain entry as much as you will need the votes of members with whom you are friendly. Hang out with more than just the member who brought you to the MC.

D. Learn everything you can about how your MC rides and how to be competent while riding in the pack with them. The movement of the pack is the most important aspect of getting the MC from one point to another. It needs to look good while operating efficiently. You need to become a top operator while riding in the pack.

E. Learn your MC's bylaws. If you are not a scholar of your MC's bylaws by the time you crossover, you have failed.

F. Learn how to escort and protect the President and other MC dignitaries. If harm comes to the President on your watch, you have failed.

G. Learn the political players in your chapter and decide where your political affiliations will lie after you crossover. But NEVER take a political position in the MC while you are prospecting. You are there for the MC, not for any side one way or the other. You are there for the President and legally elected officers. Prospects should never take sides in internal MC wars. You are only a Prospect and therefore you have no opinion on politics. Never take sides. That will always backfire against you because you have to win 100% of the vote to crossover and taking sides can create enemies in your MC that you may never overcome. Remember you are there for the whole MC only. As a Prospect, remain neutral.

H. Make yourself available to help out every time the MC needs manpower. Always volunteer—never wait to be asked.

I. Keep the clubhouse clean. Allow no full patched brother to lift a hand to clean something before you handle that task. Full patched brothers should never have to clean a surface, lift a box or wash a bike when you are near.

J. Stock the bar and serve behind the bar while you are in the clubhouse.

K. Watch over the brothers' bikes while on runs.

L. Watch over the parking lots and stand duty at the door to control the crowds during MC events.

M. Protect the MC's women or properties while on The Set.

N. Send out a daily text message to the full patched brothers when you are available to get on your bike and run errands the MC may require. Do this when you get off of work or on a Saturday morning or Sunday afternoon when the MC may not be engaged in a function. There will always be a brother who needs to have an errand run.

O. Make yourself available to help any brother you know is working on his bike. You will learn a lot about bike maintenance and every brother can use a helping hand to pass a wrench or would appreciate assistance out of a tight spot you may know more about.

P. Sit outside of the hospital rooms of sick or injured full patched brothers. The MC is well represented when a brother's family can see a guard sitting outside a brother's door to give him any assistance he may need. This kind of service to the MC is always greatly appreciated. Even as a National President, I have spent countless hours sitting outside of hospital rooms or sitting inside of them.

Q. Visit sick or injured full patched brothers at home to see about their wellbeing and run errands.

R. Ride to every chapter within your region and introduce yourself personally to the members on their church day or bike night. You will receive great respect from your regional MC Nation. They will know you get out on the scoot and putt!

> "Hello I'm Prospect X of the Atlanta chapter and I wanted to ride down to introduce myself and get to know you all."

S. Call Presidents of chapters outside of your region and introduce yourself. Ride to those chapters as well, if you can. You have brothers all across America who wear your patch and live by your code. It's a feeling of family you will never forget.

Nuts and Bolts

Your prospectship should have a set of goals that define your mission which should not only be to win your colors but to become as knowledgeable about your MC's culture, history, brothers and protocols as humanly possible before you crossover. If you are a slacker your goal will simply be to survive the prospectship just to get your colors. If you are that slacker you are a waste of everyone's time including your own. Imagine what it would be like to finally be voted in as a member of your MC and not even know what the symbols and meanings of the colors on your back represent. Imagine not knowing the year your MC was founded or the names of the Original Seven founding fathers. Many Prospects allow themselves to be voted into a MC without knowing the government names of their MC brothers. You don't want to be on the side of the rode with your brother who has been involved in an accident and the paramedic asks you his given name and your answer being "Top Dog Rider, heck I don't know his real name?" How ridiculous is that? Unfortunately, it happens every day. Don't make your prospectship a waste of time. Think of your prospectship as a job that you need to get done. Invest the time in your prospectship into accomplishing that job. Your rewards will be exceptional.

Following a Friend into the MC

Consider why you want to Prospect for the MC. Is it because your friend thought it was a good thing to do and did not want to do it alone so he asked you to come? If you want to Prospect for the MC because your friend is prospecting for the MC then you will leave the MC because your friend decides to leave the MC. You are not joining a brotherhood to be one of our brothers. Instead you are a follower experimenting with something the rest of us hold dear. Stay home! We don't need followers who can't think with their own minds. We don't need prospective brothers who can't join us with the intention of spending the rest of their lives explicitly tied to us at the hip. We would rather not love you, trust you, teach you, confide in you, train you, assist you, counsel you, depend upon you and bond with you when you know that in the end, you won't dwell among us. Part from us now and know us not! Don't involve yourself with us. You are no good to us! We are in this for an eternity. This is more than just a Motorcycle Club to us. It is a brotherhood upon which we have formed our way of life! Never follow a friend into a MC. Go there because it is who you are or who you want to be.

Your Woman and the MC

The MC life is difficult for civilian women to understand. If your woman is not on The Set, keep her as far from it as time and space will allow. A wholesome woman not familiar with the shenanigans of our ilk is seldom able to understand your love for the MC. It will be foreign to her. She won't accept it and will wonder what mid-life crisis or other personality disorder may be affecting you.

Case Study 11: Losing your Woman

Her name was Tarita. I loved her as she was everything beautiful my world knew and I loved her with all of my being. When she left me, chief among her reasons was my leadership of the Mighty Black Sabbath Motorcycle Club Nation.

The MC life is different from the life civilians know. There are rules and protocols that civilians think we are crazy for swearing to uphold. Many women will find this dedication to this new group of men baffling and frightening. She will feel threatened by the competition between the MC and herself for your time. Keep it mystical. Keep it to yourself. Keep it away from her. After all, these are guys you are just now getting to know yourself, so how can you know what type of behavior they may exhibit in front of your woman to make her question your good sense, good character and good judgment? A woman who is not a "Set Girl" will find it difficult to understand the MC life. So don't involve her. Let it be that thing you do by yourself when you go do your thing with the fellows.

Case Study 12: Women Often Don't Understand the MC

One of my brothers once took a picture of my woman's butt when she was getting off of the back of my bike. He thought it was so funny, but she wanted blood. This kind of prank can run rampant in the "boys will be boys" arena in which the MC life is played. It left her with a permanent distaste for the MC. He committed an offense for which she never forgave me. And in that simple thoughtless prank he added one more reason for her to dislike and mistrust the MC. If you have the kind of woman who will not tolerate this kind of stupidity why expose her to it?

On the other hand if the MC consumes your entire life and you immerse yourself totally within it then she will have no choice but to become a part of it because, like me, it will be a major component of your life. Then you will have to break her in slowly, protecting her and explaining to her every step of the way what she is seeing and why things are occurring. Don't be surprised if she opts out. She can also opt out of dealing with the MC while deciding to simultaneously stay with you, which can make real hell at home because she will continually make you decide between her and the MC at every level.

Case Study 13: Her or the MC

One of our brothers threw himself into the MC from the first day of his prospectship. He was riding in the pack competently on his first day as a hang-around and was capable of leading the pack as a Road Captain before he even put on his Prospect patch. He was at every club meeting, on every run with zest, enthusiasm and excitement. Soon he started bringing his wife on our journeys and at first everything was great. Then the MC started going through a period of fighting amongst ourselves. On the day she went on a run where there was nearly a fist fight between two brothers, she had finally had enough of the MC. For him, we were family and he knew he had found his home despite how much she disliked the MC. He was going to be with us forever. She; however, made sure that she would almost never be in public with our erratic butts again. So whenever he wanted to hang out with the MC, first, there was a fight at home. She was not going and did not want him to go either. So she made it very difficult for him and his participation decreased dramatically. She often made him decide—her or the MC.

Make sure you know the MC before you try to bring your significant other around. Prospect first, become a full patched brother, learn what you need to protect her from and include her in before unleashing the mighty MC upon her. You might not want to bring her to the clubhouse on the nights strippers are there. Few civilian women will understand. You might not want to discuss the MC war going on between MCs or the two Prospects shot while you are on the phone around her. She is only going to wonder why a grown man would be involved in any activity that might cost him his life— even if your MC had nothing to do with it. She can figure out that your MC could be in the crossfire if there is trouble on The Set. It is not wise to discuss your whorish brother, who changes women like he changes motor oil in his bike with her. She won't find that funny and will only wonder when his inappropriate behavior will negatively affect you—especially since you are so enthralled with this new leader in your life. She will wonder how long it will be before you are cheating on your woman too. So the best rule of thumb is to keep MC business inside the MC and limit her exposure to any negative thing that could detract from your relationship with her or cheapen her respect of you and the MC.

Your Best Friend and Friends vs. the MC

It is easy to want to look cool in your new Prospect colors and ride around all of your friends as the new bad-ass on the block. Resist this temptation. The MC is private and its business is not to be discussed among your friends and displayed as a boasting topic. They are not prospective brothers of the mighty MC, you are. Most people who are trying to look tough or show off accomplish neither. If your best friend wants to know about the MC life you can easily educate him by suggesting he buy a motorcycle and hang around. Other than that there is not much you can or should tell him— especially when it comes to the business of your MC. You could always buy him a copy of this book. It will serve as a good starting point for his education.

Beware— friends can be jealous when it comes to feeling threatened by your association with the MC. They can feel like you have forgotten them and start to compete for your time just like a jilted girlfriend. Treat friends appropriately and prepare them for your new journey. Let them know you are joining a brotherhood and that you will be taking on new brothers and not to be worried because you still love them. Sometimes friends need to be told this so they are not threatened as you move onto another phase of your life. Best friends often feel like they are your brothers and won't take kindly to you creating a new set of best friends. They can sense that you may be moving forward. Value your friendships and provide them with the nourishment they need so they won't feel the need to compete with your love of the MC for attention.

Your Job and the MC

There is always that guy who shows up to the job adorned in Prospect colors and wonders why he got fired. If you have not figured it out yet wearing colors is not something done by most of society. Equally wearing colors is not seen as a great and noble thing by most employers. We are not 1%ers. We are 99%ers and we need our jobs. Keep your colors on your bike. You don't need to wear them to work. You should also be careful about wearing them when you leave work. You might not want to put them on in the parking lot. Instead wait till you get a far enough away from the job that it is okay to wear them. Civilians don't know the difference between 1%ers and 99%ers. They won't understand your colors so don't put that on them. Don't make your employer see you as the gang member guy with poor judgment. It might not cost you your job but instead your promotion. As always keep MC business to yourself. If by chance you work in one of those places where it does not matter, wear your colors and be happy. If you don't know whether or not it would matter—don't wear them to the job.

Loved Ones and Down-Talking the MC

Don't down-talk the MC in front of loved ones or you can expect them to hate the MC even when you are no longer mad. Loved ones will never know or understand your love for the MC. After all, not everyone has a need to wear a patch on their back as an identifier or statement of who they are. Many loved ones will think you are a bit crazy to wear a patch in the first place. You won't help things when you talk negatively about your MC to loved ones—especially wives, girlfriends and mothers. Fathers, brothers and uncles tend to better understand the "boys will be boys" and/or militaristic atmosphere of a MC.

Loved ones love you fiercely and after you have forgiven the MC for wronging you it is likely that your brother, mother, sister and/or wife never will. In fact your loved one may grow to passionately hate the MC forever for doing something to you that no longer makes you angry.

A sure way to get your loved ones to hate the MC is to down-talk the MC or handle negative MC business on the phone in front of them. If their only experience with your MC is to see you arguing on the phone, they will begin to wonder the good of the MC for you.

They will find ways to resist your decisions to go to MC events and even attempt to make you decide between spending time with the MC or them. Wives and girlfriends may especially take it upon themselves to destroy your relationship with the MC by intentionally keeping you away. A girlfriend once told me that she was praying for God to take me out of the MC. What MC can compete with God?

No Bike, No MC

Why would you want to join a MC if you don't have a motorcycle? Are you some kind of groupie? I despise you. Your kind weakens the MC. With no bike to ride all you can do is sit around the clubhouse and gossip like old women. You cause hate and stir up consternation, grief and discontent. Why!? Why not get a motorcycle? Is the feel of the MC life so grand that it is worth mimicking? The M in MC stands for "Motorcycle". The C stands for "Club". That means you need a MOTORCYCLE to be in the CLUB.

If you want to belong to a traditional MC you should never approach them without having your bike in hand.

Not,

"I am getting one soon."

Not,

"I wrecked my bike and I am just waiting for the insurance to pay off."

Not,

"I am injured right now and I am waiting for my settlement so I can't ride until I settle my claim because I am really not supposed to be riding and I am hiding out from the insurance investigators."

Not,

Any of this nonsense.

Approach the MC with a motorcycle, a license and the ability to contribute as a riding Prospect capable of representing the MC on two (the two means two wheels)! Every tradesman needs to have his tools. As a Prospect, your tools are your bike, a willing attitude towards service to the MC, an open mind and a desire to represent the MC. Bring them with you to work. The job is your prospectship.

Even though a traditional MC should never allow you to Prospect without a motorcycle, many are doing that very thing just to get numbers up. It is a sad commentary on the many failings of MCs today. Don't be that guy! Have more pride than that! When I prospected twenty-four years ago I showed up with a bike, a license and a willingness to serve. Not having a bike would have been unheard of! You should feel the same way.

Bike Maintenance – The Gospel According to Bob Schultz

It is your responsibility to keep your bike well maintained. You should check the air pressure in your tires once per week. Take measurements of your tire tread biweekly. Check your chain tightness once per week. Keep your maintenance records and oil changes up to date. Keep your insurance and license plates up to date. Don't be the one whose chain fell off in the middle of the pack and caused everyone's motorcycle to crash behind you.

Case Study 14: My Chain Fell Off in the Pack

In California, 1997, my poorly maintained chain snapped off at high speed, nearly taking my bike down along with the rest of the pack behind me. It took a long time for the pack to forgive me for that one!

Make the Difference

One hard riding Prospect can turn a declining MC on its heels. Be that Prospect! One man can make the difference. Be that one man! Wake up every day looking to see what you can do within the MC to improve its condition. Ride hard and others will follow.

A Prospect should never whine. Look around to see what needs to be done. No one should have to tell you to pick up a broom or help a brother put a bike up on a lift. Eagerly look for another project where you could be helpful. One day you will be full patched brother. Work hard to prove you are worthy of brotherhood. Make the difference in your MC by loving your MC more than you love yourself. Get this prayer in your head as early as you can; "It's not about me it's about my MC and my brothers and sisters within my MC." The sooner you can recite this prayer and mean it, the sooner you can do something outstanding and worthwhile for the MC.

When other members see your enthusiasm they become enthusiastic as well. They liven up and start becoming better MC members because you are a better Prospect. Being awesome makes others around you step their game up to be awesome as well. Think of how a superstar athlete inspires his teammates to make spectacular plays. Be the MC's Most Valuable Player (MVP). You can do it! It is up to you!

An enthusiastic Prospect brings new members to the MC. He talks about his MC to quality people he would like to see as MC brothers; people he wants in his MC. When you start making a difference by recruiting, full patched brothers will start recruiting too.

Be the one that makes a difference simply by doing what is right for the MC every time someone looks your way.

You are the MC

Just like one man can turn the MC around for the good, one man can also destroy the MC. You represent every person across the nation that wears our cut, every time you put it on. One misstep could have you on the front page of a national magazine—and that means we (the MC) will be on that front page too, which could, in effect, force every member of the MC to have to take their colors off. Be responsible and think of others before you do something stupid, illegal or thoughtless in our rags.

Running Alone

The Biker Set can be a dangerous place. You can put your safety in jeopardy when you interfere in another MC's business. Make damned sure you can stand when you decide to take a stance because a mistake may cost you your life. You won't carry the respect of a full patched brother when you are alone on The Set. People may try you. Be capable of handling yourself and make wise decisions if you decide to go it alone.

Case Study 15: Thank God for Zulu and Route 66 MC

I was a Prospect for a long time before I ever got it right. So, I rode alone quite a bit. It is easy to get into trouble when you run alone as a Prospect because you really don't know what you are doing and you don't have the respect of full patched brothers of other MCs. You have to be careful and use common sense. I was in East Los Angeles when I rode up to a MC clubhouse, by myself at 3:00 in the morning, a hundred miles from home. The brothers of that MC were known to be particularly tough but I was ignorant Prospect and new to the Bike Set, so there was no place that was off limits. A man walked by with his little puppy and one of the girls screamed when she saw this four month old dog, acting like it was going to kill her. The man tried to apologize and move along with his dog, but one of the full patched brothers of that MC took the opportunity to look tough and pulled out his knife to stab and kill the puppy. I was not going to let that animal get murdered so off my bike I leapt. The man moved before I did and stood between the full patched brother and his puppy. The biker then sucker punched the man and knocked him out cold. The man actually fell into the street from the curb and laid out snoring. I knew he was going to be run over and killed as cars were moving down that street at 60 mph and could not see him in time to stop. All of the clubhouse patrons were standing there partying like nothing had happened with the man lying in the street about to be run over. So I ran over to him, grabbed him by the legs and drug him out of the street. Now, as a Prospect I had interfered in their MC's business. And so it was on and popping! I noticed that I was being surrounded for this obvious violation of MC protocol. I was not going to go down with the sucker punch so I squared up on the closet guy. It was my plan to stab him in the throat with so much violence that I might be able to get a break in the circle from which to attempt to flee but before I could put my half-hearted plan in motion, a group of brothers from Route 66 MC broke through the circle and grabbed me up. The leader's name was 'Zulu'. He said, "Come on Prospect, it's time for you to get on your bike and take yourself back home to San Diego!" His brothers were shoulder to shoulder all around me and they walked me through the circle of that angry MC, to my bike and put me on it. They stood there while I started it and then each one got on his bike separately and rode up to surround me until they were all on their bikes. They opened up the circle and allowed me to ride out and they rode me out of that Los Angeles neighborhood. I will never forget Zulu for that! I want publically say "Thank you, Zulu and Route 66 MC!"

The Last Rev

The passing of a fellow MC brother or sister is something we never hope to have to endure. The reality of it is if you live long enough that day will come. There is a tradition within the MC culture that has been around for many years, called "The Last Rev". The Road Captain, while standing beside his bike, starts his engine then everyone standing beside their bike starts their engines, the Road

Captain starts the rev three to five times with everyone else joining in and doing the same except the tail gunner who just waits until everyone else has finished. When the Road Captain stops the rev and all bikes are just idling, the Tail Gunner gives the last rev then everyone mounts their bikes and rides away as quiet as possible. Normally, "The Last Rev" is done at the cemetery unless there will be no cemetery service, and then it will be done at the funeral home after the last viewing just prior to everyone leaving.

The significance of this is to alert heaven that a Biker is on their way to ride the roads in heaven. There may be variations to this ceremony between MCs but the purpose is still the same. Learn the ceremony so you will know how to conduct yourself.

Grave Tending

I believe that Benjamin Franklin once said, "One can tell the morals of a culture by the way they treat their dead."

It is customary to tend the grave sites of brothers who have passed on before us. They carried our torches long before many of us ever even heard of the MC Nation. Their graves will therefore be tended while we are living. During the grave tending ceremony, the MC will often gather and pour some wine or other favorite beverage at the deceased's head stone. I have also witnessed the burying of a joint or blunt if the deceased was particularly fond of such a partaking. During the grave tending ceremony, the grave site is cleaned and tidied. Weeds are pulled and the area is given a general sprucing. Prayers may be spoken and stories are often told of what the member meant to the MC or to individuals with whom he shared the MC's brotherhood. You may be sent as a Prospect to tend to passed members' grave sites. Always undertake this task with great reverence. Tend to your deceased brothers' graves like you would want yours to be tended.

Don't Speak Ill of Brothers Former or Present

Always remember that other brothers were passionate about the MC Nation long before you—some even before you were old enough to know what a motorcycle was. These brothers lived, loved, breathed, fought, bled and sweat the MC's reputation. They shouted our great name to the magnificent heavens and bayed before God on moonlit nights, resting on lonely highways. Though your passion is great, Prospect, remember that your passion is new here. You are new blood, new to the MC game, new to the struggle, new to the brotherhood and new to your chosen MC's way of life— even if you come from another MC, you are still new to this one. So, EARN the right to open your mouth before you open it. Never speak negatively about your newly found MC Nation and certainly never speak ill about the full patched brothers who went before you and made the sacrifices necessary for you to ride today, You will earn the right to speak after you crossover. Until such time remain silent! You need to learn what's going on before speaking.

Never speak ill of your MC publically or on any social media. Never speak ill of your brothers, past or present. When you speak of your forefathers speak in hushed tones of respect, love and admiration. Whatever their sins may have been, they held those colors down so that one day in the future – you could as well!

John E. Bunch II 'Black Dragon' BSFFBS

Case Study 16: Speaking Negatively, Publically About a Brother

I had the unfortunate experience of seeing a load of angry posts on a social media site about a deceased brother's cut being sold on the internet. The auctioneer boasted about how the cut was owned by a former member of a true biker gang. It caused great anger among the brothers of the MC because they felt that even though the cut no longer bore the turtle shell it was just as painful to see it for sale. I made it clear that I would get to the bottom of it when one of our Prospects posted, "No matter what the cause this man is a piece of shit for what he did!" Immediately, one of our Sisters of the Cross posted that this brother had died, abandoned in a nursing home, two years prior so he had nothing to do with that overseas internet auction.

As I thought of an appropriate punishment for the Prospect, I realized that he was just trying to be passionate about his MC. Unfortunately, his passion was misplaced.

Chapter 4

Outlaw 1% MCs/OMGs

The Outlaw Motorcycle Club (OMC) is a dominant part of biker society that can't be ignored, underestimated, disrespected or taken lightly. To do so could prove hazardous to your health and that of your brothers so learn how to deal with the 1%er MCs. Simply put, it is what it is and it has been this way for nearly one hundred years.

What is an OMC

An OMC is a MC Set subculture. Its members ride mostly American made cruiser motorcycles, particularly Harley-Davidsons and custom built choppers with American made engines. They follow a set of protocols which are centered on freedom, nonconformity to mainstream culture and loyalty to the MC. In the United States, such Motorcycle Clubs are considered "outlaw" as they are not sanctioned by the AMA and do not adhere to the AMA's rules or bylaws. Instead OMCs abide by their own bylaws, values and culture. Some OMCs claim territory, which is often the name of the state from which they operate, as part of their colors or on their bottom rockers. There are exceptions to this as there are OMCs that do not have their state as part of their colors.

WARNING: 99%er MCs do not claim states as territory and do not wear state bottom rockers!

John E. Bunch II 'Black Dragon' BSFFBS

How Did Outlaw MCs Begin

In 1924, the American Motorcyclist Association (AMA) began sanctioning MCs and quickly established themselves as the governing body for MCs across America. There were other sanctioning bodies before the AMA, but eventually they all merged.[1] MCs that were not sanctioned by the AMA and did not adhere to their rules became known as Outlaw Motorcycle Clubs.[2]

WWII Vets' Influence on Modern Outlaw MC

Returning vets from World War II began filling the ranks of OMCs to relive the camaraderie they experienced in their wartime units and to ease the pressures of rejoining society from which many vets felt estranged.[3] These vets often suffered from, then called "battle fatigue"[4] or "shell shock,"[5] now called post-traumatic stress disorder (PTSD).[6] OMCs provided these returning soldiers with the support and brotherhood government agencies could not provide. Brothers who had experienced the same atrocities of war and could relate to them. This culture and sense of brotherhood rubbed off and OMCs began to operate from a set of protocols that closely

---

[1] The history of the AMA merged with pre-existing sanctioning bodies is an interesting read and I would encourage you to check out http://www.americanmotorcyclist.com to learn their history.
[2] (American Motorcyclist Association) see bibliography
[3] (WikiPedia) see bibliography
[4] (Wikipedia) see bibliography
[5] (Wikipedia) see bibliography
[6] (Wikipedia Post Traumatic Stress Disorder) see bibliography

resembled their war time military units in organization, operation and discipline.[7]

At that time, OMCs usually rode inexpensive American made motorcycles, most often Harley Davidsons. Some rode chopped Japanese manufactured motorcycles they practically hand built out of spare parts. Their protocols celebrated freedom, nonconformity to society and loyalty to the MC.

The Hollister Riot

OMCs did not always conduct themselves in a way that was appealing to the AMA at their AMA-sponsored events causing animosity to build up between conformists and nonconformists. This animosity was fueled by news reporters of the time who wanted to create a rift they could write about to sell newspapers. The Hollister riot occurred at an AMA-sanctioned Gypsy Tour motorcycle rally in Hollister, California from July 3 – 6, 1947. Many more motorcyclists than expected flooded the small town to watch the annual rallies, socialize and drink. A few of the motorcyclists got out of control and caused a commotion in the town—although at the end of the event, the damage was considered minor. This incident became known as the "Hollister riot", was sensationalized by the press with reports of bikers "taking over the town" and "pandemonium" in Hollister. The strongest dramatization of the event was a staged photo of a drunken man sitting on a motorcycle surrounded by beer bottles. It was published in *LIFE* magazine, bringing national attention and negative criticism

---

[7] (WikiPedia) see biblography

to the event. The Hollister riot helped to give rise to the image of the outlaw biker.[8]

1%er

The effect of the idea of biker hoodlums looting towns at AMA events was quite unsettling to post WWII United States society facing a looming Cold War. Though newspapers needed a good selling story and sensationalized negative coverage, the AMA did not want its reputation tarnished so it has been rumored that the AMA released a statement indicating they had no involvement with the Hollister riot, and "The trouble was caused by the one percent deviant that tarnishes the public image of both motorcycles and motorcyclists" and that the other ninety-nine percent of motorcyclists are good, decent, law-abiding citizens.[9] Outlaw Motorcycle Club Nations took on the designation and began proudly calling themselves 1%er MCs and the culture of the OMC was forever changed.

AMA Denies 1%er Claim

The AMA has no record of ever releasing such a statement. A representative of the AMA said in 2005, "We've been unable to attribute [the term 1%er] original use to an AMA official or published statement — so it's apocryphal." Since this statement, which led to the term 1%er being widely used to describe outlaw motorcycle clubs and motorcyclists, has been denied as being

---

[8] (WikiPedia Hollister Riot) see bibliography
[9] (WikiPedia Hollister Riot) see bibliography

authored by the AMA, it may never be known how this term came to be.

Outlaw Motorcycle Gangs (OMG)

Theoretically, any MC that does not conform to AMA rules and regulations is considered an OMC by the AMA. However, many law enforcement agencies only view 1%er Outlaw Motorcycle Gangs (OMGs) as criminal. Therefore, the OMG classification has been established to identify MCs that engage in criminal activities and organized crime. These MCs are seen by law enforcement agencies as being unique among groups that carry out crimes because they maintain websites, identify themselves through patches and tattoos, have written constitutions and bylaws, trademark their MC names and logos, and even carry out publicity campaigns aimed at cleaning up their public images.[10]

DOJ Vs OMCs/OMGs

On its website, the Department of Justice (DOJ) defines OMGs as: "Organizations whose members use their motorcycle clubs as conduits for criminal enterprise." The site further states OMGs are highly structured criminal organizations whose members engage in criminal activities such as violent crime, weapons trafficking, and drug trafficking. The DOJ claims there are more than three hundred active OMGs within the United States, ranging in size from single chapters with five or six members to hundreds of chapters with thousands of members worldwide. It names the Hells Angels,

---

[10] (Wikipedia Outlaw Motorcycle Clubs) see bibliography

Mongols, Bandidos, Outlaws, and Sons of Silence as MCs that pose a serious national domestic threat and conduct the majority of criminal activity linked to OMGs, especially activity relating to drug-trafficking and, more specifically, to cross-border drug smuggling. It claims that because of their transnational scope, these OMGs are able to coordinate drug smuggling operations in partnership with major international drug-trafficking organizations (DTOs).

ATF Classifies OMC/OMG

The Bureau of Alcohol Tobacco and Fire Arms (ATF) defines 1%er OMGs/OMCs as "any group of motorcyclists who have voluntarily made a commitment to band together to abide by their organization's rules enforced by violence and who engage in activities that bring them and their club into repeated and serious conflict with society and the law. The group must be an ongoing organization, association of three or more persons which have a common interest and/or activity characterized by the commission of or involvement in a pattern of criminal or delinquent conduct." The ATF estimates there are approximately three hundred 1%er OMGs in the United States.

Support Clubs

OMGs have many organizations that support their efforts. Local Motorcycle Club Associations (MCAs), supporter MCs, satellite clubs and social clubs take up the causes of the dominant MCs and often champion their agendas. You can recognize the supporter organizations because they wear the support patches of their supported OMGs. Their support patches will display something like: "Support Club of the #### MC".

Is Your MC a Support Club

You will be able to tell by observing the patches on your MCs cuts, but make sure to ask. Know the requirements for your MC as a supporter club and that you are able to adequately handle these requirements, should you become a member. Are you prepared to go to war with that OMG should it face an enemy if this is required of you?

What is a Dominant OMC

A dominant OMC/OMG is the most powerful 1%er MC in a particular area. This may be because it is the oldest OMC in that area or because it has fought to win the territory and taken it over. Sometimes it is simply because it has the most members and is too big to be challenged.

What Does the Dominant 1%er Control

The dominant MC in an area, 1%er or 99%er, will control the MCs that exist in that area. It will bless new MCs and allow them to operate unmolested or may blackball a MC and forbid it to operate at all in its territory. It may also settle disputes between warring MCs within its boundaries to keep conflict to a minimum therefore minimizing law enforcement activity on the Biker Set. The dominant MC will be respected and exert its authority. If it is disrespected it can resort to great physical violence which can leave dead bodies in its wake. As a Prospect it is not wise for you to engage 1%ers alone except to exchange greetings and show respect. Don't try to act tough around them or attempt to make a name for yourself by saying something stupid or trying to look like a know it all. That tactic will most often backfire and you could find yourself extremely embarrassed.

MCs that Stand in Defiance to the Dominant

Sure, sometimes a 99%er MC decides that it won't tolerate the scrutiny of a 1%er dominant MC. Perhaps the dominant has disrespected the 99%er MC or maybe it has decided to shut down the 99%er's bike night or maybe it won't let the 99%er open a new chapter in its jurisdiction. There could be lots of reasons for a rift. If you are prospecting for a 99%er MC that is warring with a 1%er dominant MC, be sure you understand exactly what you are up against. Most 99%er MCs simply don't have the manpower to spar with a 1%er dominant MC Nation. Your MC may win the battle but lose the war.

How to Identify 1%er MCs

Most 1%er MCs will wear a diamond shaped patch on the front of their cuts. In many cases that diamond will have a "1%er" or a "1" inside of it, but there can be many other numbers other than that inside of the diamond or no numbers at all. Sometimes there is a number that represents letters of the alphabet. For instance there could be a number "13" inside the diamond, representing the letter "M" which could represent MC, murder, methamphetamines or many other things. When you see that diamond you know you are dealing with a 1%er no matter what number may be in that diamond.

The back patch of an OMC will normally be in three pieces. This Setup is known as a three-piece patch:

- The top piece (or top rocker) will indicate the MC's name
- The center piece will be the MC's symbol or icon
- The bottom rocker will name the MC's state

Note: A five-piece patch is sometimes worn with the letters "M" and "C" split apart.

Note: Not all 1%er MCs Nations have three-piece or five-piece patches. There are some OMC that have only a one-piece back patch with no state rocker at all. You might not always be able to tell by looking from the back but seeing that diamond on the front should alert you that you are looking at a 1%er.

Note: Many 99%er MCs Nations wear three-piece and five-piece patches. The three-piece or five-piece patch is not the sole identifying characteristic of a 1%er MC, Nation just like a one-piece patch is not the sole identifying characteristic of a 99%er MC Nation. If you see a one-piece patch MC wearing a diamond on the front of their cuts you will know that you are in the company of a 1%er MC. A three-piece patch of a 99%er MC will never have a bottom state rocker.

Surrendering Your Colors

There are certain situations that you may encounter when a 1%er MC or a 1%er supporter club may try to remove your colors from your back. There could be many reasons. Anything from you shouldn't have passed them in formation on the highway to your MC is unrecognized or not blessed to operate in certain geographical area. Or maybe they just don't like your MC and want to intimidate the hell out of you. Whether or not you are going to surrender your colors is a decision that you need to make, long before you are faced with the possibility of having to do so. No man can tell you that you should NEVER take off your colors and surrender them to anyone and that you should die on the street for those colors. I can only advise you as to the options you have and then let the decision ride with you and your brothers. As a Prospect take the clues from your full patched brothers if confronted. If you are alone you will have to think on your own.

Ask about your MC's policy when it comes to surrendering your colors to 1%ers or anyone else who might demand them, such as law enforcement. If your MC is strictly a riding club or hobby club, the policy could simply be, "Surrender those colors and we'll give you some more when you get back home." Fair enough. It is up to you to know that kind of information in advance. You don't want to find yourself scrapping for your life over colors that your brothers would not be fighting alongside you to keep because to do so would be against the MC policy. I'm also not going to sit here and type to you that I have not seen the hardest bad-ass characters keep their colors when the situation was totally against them and their lives were in jeopardy. But I have also seen a couple of them give up colors and walk away.

1%ers a Prospect's Take Away

So what do you need to know as a Prospect? You need to know that these things can happen. You need to know how your MC wants these things to be handled. You need to know if you have the kind of MC that will back you if the chips get flakey and by "flakey" I mean Really Flakey. You need to know in your own heart and mind if you are willing to kill, go to prison, get a criminal record or have to spend the rest of your life looking over your shoulder or die based on a set of colors. And you need to decide if all of this is even for you. Only then will you be able to handle the situation appropriately should it occur and you are placed in a position where you have to confront it.

Chapter 5

How are MCs Organized

Most traditional MCs are setup similarly making it easy to identify members and their status within the MC Nations.

National MCs with Multiple Chapters

A 99%er law abiding Motorcycle Club Nation with multiple chapters will likely have a committee of elected and/or appointed officers who oversee the national business of the MC Nation. National MCs are generally thought of as having five chapters in at least three states, but I have seen clubs with as few as two chapters in one state that elect or appoint a National President. In a 99%er law abiding National Motorcycle Club these offices are common:

- National President
- National Vice President
- High Council President
- National Sgt-at-Arms or National Enforcer
- Regional Presidents
- National Ambassador
- Nomad

Note: Enforcers are generally thought of as existing in 1%er Motorcycle Club Nations; however, some 99%er law abiding Motorcycle Club Nations have them as well.

Local Chapters

Officers make up the committee or council in local chapters and run the daily functions of the local chapter. The local chapter of a traditional MC may have all or some of the following offices. There is a hierarchy as follows:

- President
- Vice President
- Sgt-at-Arms
- Road Captain
- Secretary
- Treasurer

These positions may or may not be present or may vary in ranking:

- Public Relations Officer (PRO)
- Business Manager
- Prospect Coordinator

Non Officers

- Full Patched Brothers
- Honorary Members
- Prospects
- Female Social Club / Property / House Mommas
- Support Crew (men members who have no bikes)
- Hang-arounds

Responsibilities of Offices

It is important that you know the responsibilities of the officers that are over you. In your MC career you may hold some or all of these titles.

National President

Elected or appointed by committee. The National President is the servant of the MC Nation. It is his responsibility to use his authority to carry out the MC Nation's desires according to the vote of the MC's democratic system. The National President is the spokesman of the MC Nation. He is the highest ranking officer in the MC Nation. In some MC Nations the National President can be overturned by the High Council in a special vote; however, this is not a common occurrence.

National Vice President

Elected or appointed by committee. The National Vice President is the details oriented officer who ensures the National President's directives are accomplished in accordance to the MC Nation's bylaws.

High Council President

The High Council is made up of the President and Vice President of every local chapter. The High Council President convenes the High Council meetings to ensure they are conducted in an orderly manner. When convened, the High Council votes and presents its vote to the National President who does not vote except to break a tie. In this way the National President will know the MC Nation's desires and will then carry them out.

National Sgt-at-Arms

Elected or appointed by committee. The National Sergeant at Arms (Sgt-at-Arms) ensures the MC Nation's national bylaws are followed by the chapters and that local bylaws are administered correctly by local Sgt-at-Arms. He handles disciplinary matters escalated from the local chapters to the national level, ensures the protection and security of the National President and other national officers and trains the local chapter Sgts-at-Arms to carry out their duties.

Regional President

Elected or appointed by committee. The Regional President is the servant of the MCs within his jurisdiction. He is the highest ranking officer in his specific area of operation. He manages the local chapters within his region and convenes the regional councils to make decisions for his geographical area of responsibility and then accomplishes their desires.

Nomad/Enforcer

Normally appointed by the National President, the Nomad or Enforcer travels from chapter to chapter under the direction of the National President to squelch local issues and mete out disciplinary actions. He may also spearhead solving problems with outside MCs, Local and Regional Presidents before issues get out of hand and rise to a national conflict level.

These responsibilities can also be accomplished by the National Sgt-at-Arms.

Responsibilities of Local Officers

The following are the responsibilities of the officers within your local chapter:

President

The President is the highest elected office in the MC. He is the servant and the spokesman of the MC chapter. His job is to carry out the will of his chapter communicated to him via a club vote or by committee. The President never participates in a club vote except to break a tie.

Vice President

The Vice President is the second highest office in the MC and as such works hand-in-hand with the President to accomplish the MC's agenda. He accepts responsibility for the President in his absence. He oversees the day-to-day operations and internal 'running' of the MC. He has in-depth knowledge of the details of every officer's reports, status, level of training, roll call, MC events, runs, activities, finances and MC business. He ensures all junior officers are trained to perform their duties. The Vice President will take over leadership of the MC if the President is incapacitated or can no longer perform his duties.

Sgt-at-Arms

The Sergeant-at-Arms (Sgt-at-Arms) is third in command and third in succession to the President. The Sgt-at-Arms is in charge of the security of the MC. He is also responsible for enforcing the MC's bylaws, fines, punishments and ensuring the discipline of the MC. He maintains orderly conduct during club meetings and ensures all members are aware of MC participation in time-scheduled events. He makes sure members are present for the count on MC runs at annual dances, notifies the Vice President of all imposed fines and keeps a record of all fines and penalties.

Note: In some MC's the Sgt-at-Arms is the only member authorized to use physical force against a member or Prospect in the MC—to maintain/reestablish order at club meetings, confiscate colors or officer insignia, break up fights between members and/or maintain the peace of the MC. He may deputize any available members needed to accomplish this end.

The Sgt-at-Arms is responsible for the security of the President on runs and may deputize Prospects or other members to provide security.

Road Captain

The Road Captain is responsible for moving the MC pack from point-to-point safely, efficiently and in all things keeping the MC looking good on the road. The Road Captain will most likely be the one teaching Prospects how to ride in the pack or will assign a full patched brother to teach you. He will ensure that Prospects know the correct hand signals and other tools the MC uses to move down the road as a unit. He is responsible for inspecting all motorcycles for safety, insurance, license plates, tires and any other issues that may affect bike riding in the MC pack. In many MCs. the Road Captain is the President while the pack is on the road and turns the MC back over to the President after the pack reaches its destination. On runs the Road Captain assigns the route of travel and knows how many miles each bike can get to a tank of gas before the pack has to stop for fuel. The Road Captain will likely be the best or one of the best riders in the MC. In some MCs the Road Captain has the ability to fine unruly riders while the pack is on the road.

Secretary

The Secretary is in charge of the MC's administration and correspondence. He takes minutes during church, issues correspondence between MCs and oversees all MC generated correspondence, logos, branding and other public facing MC documents.

In some MCs, Public Relations Officers (PRO) have emerged in the last few years to take over the public marketing and MC-to-MC communication responsibilities from the Secretary.

Business Manager

The Business Manager is responsible for the MC's business affairs, contracts, agreements and financial dealings.

Treasurer

The Treasurer keeps track of the MCs money, handles the bank accounts and writes the checks to pay the MC's responsibilities. The Treasurer reports the status of the MC's finances at every church meeting.

Church Meetings

Club meetings (often referred to as "having church" or "going to church") are held regularly at times specified in the bylaws. Club meetings are when the MC handles business, addressing issues and concerns, distributing discipline and discussing plans for future events and club runs. During club meetings many MCs specify certain things that must occur at every club meeting:

- Prayer
- Roll Call
- Financial Report
- Reading of last club meeting's minutes
- Old Business
- New Business
- Voting
- Discipline
- Prayer
- Adjournment

In traditional MCs, Prospects do not speak during church. If you have something to say, it must be relayed through your sponsor on a piece of paper. Try not to have anything to say at all. Your prospectship is the time for you to look, learn and listen to take in all that you can while taking copious notes. Questions can be answered later by your sponsor. If you are asked to speak during a club meeting, understand that you have been allowed a great privilege and should not squander your opportunity to speak before the MC:

1. Stand up and acknowledge the President, officers, members and Prospects of the MC.
2. Introduce yourself as Prospect X.
3. Answer the question or state your business, question or concern.
4. Thank the President and the MC.
5. Sit down.

NOTE: Whenever addressing the MC as a Prospect always show the utmost respect by standing and following the guidelines above. Display your seriousness and professionalism at all times. Let your MC brothers see how serious you are about the club's business and that you do not take the MC for granted. Be humble.

As a Prospect you may not be allowed inside the entire club meeting. The MC may handle sensitive topics while you are standing outside and invite you into the club meeting at a later time.

Do Not Discuss MC Business

At some point during your prospectship and especially in church meetings, you may be privy to sensitive MC business. You must make up in your mind at an early stage that MC business is never to be discussed outside of the MC family with anyone for any reason. This means wives, girlfriends, aunts, uncles, parents or anyone else. You are being invited into an exclusive membership that is yours only. If someone has not prospected and been voted into the MC they are never entitled to know MC business for any reason, pillow partners included. If it is discovered that you have spoken about MC business chances are you will be dismissed from the MC. Also beware of discussing MC business in public places where you can be overheard. Never speak about MC business when you are drunk or on prescription medicines. Never brag about MC business to make yourself look big. Never think, for even one moment, that you can take another person into your confidence, that is not a part of your MC and trust that what you say will be held as a secret. It won't be! I guarantee that if you tell someone in secret—you will learn the hard way there are no secrets. You'll hear it again and the finger will point at you. The only way something stays a secret is if you don't talk about it.

What is MC Business?

- Anything that happens within the MC, in club meetings, or within the MC family that has not been cleared for public consumption.
- If you have a question about whether something is MC business and should not be discussed... don't discuss it!

Don't be a party to discussions where other members or Prospects are discussing MC business in the open or on the Biker Set. When you see it occurring remove yourself from the place where it is happening. If you are questioned remind the member or Prospect that you don't discuss MC business outside of the MC family and you won't be around when it is happening.

Cell Phones

Cell phones have no place in club meetings or quorums and in many cases they have no place in the clubhouse at all. They should be left in your car or turned into the Sgt-at-Arms before the club meeting and put into a non-adjoining room. Unscrupulous members can use cell phones to video or record everything said in a club meeting. These recordings can then be used to spread the MC's business or embarrass the MC on social media. As a Prospect you should never take your cell phone into a club meeting. Never record a club meeting without authorization to do so.

CHAPTER 6
THE BIKER SET

The Set

The Biker Set commonly referred to as simply *"The Set"*, is where all bikers, who adhere to MC protocol and lifestyle, hangout, interact, ride and socialize. It is a mixture of places that combine to deliver the biker experience. The Set can be at a regular hotel having a "biker weekend"-- for that weekend that hotel becomes part of The Set, or it can be at a motorcycle club that is always on The Set. The Set can be at a park or a run like Sturgis or National Biker Roundup or the thousands of rallies, races, roundups, bike weeks, gypsy runs, bike shows and charity events that happen year round. Wherever you find bikers that adhere to the MC protocol and lifestyle hanging out and having fun, you will find yourself on The Set.

Who is on the Biker Set

Participants of The Set are traditional 99%er law abiding MC Nations, female bike clubs, riding clubs, motorsports clubs, independent bikers, biker chics, groupies (male and females), hang-arounds, Prospects, civilians, gawkers, wannabes, 1% Outlaw Motorcycle Club Nations and others. These people are all somehow bound by the mystique of two wheels and are to some extent drawn to the lifestyle.

What Types of Motorcycles & People

The Set used to be primarily thought of as consisting of hard-core, Harley-riding outlaw bikers who worked as auto-mechanics during the day time and terrorized communities and villages at night, but that stereotype is not true. You can find anyone participating on The Set. Today, The Set has motorcycles from every genre from crotch rockets to cruisers, and includes people from all walks of life, professionals, blue collar workers, military personnel and trades people.

Sometimes regular motorcyclist and bikers mingle at events designed to draw two wheels, like bike shows. At these times The Biker Set and motorcyclists enter a space they seldom share. For motorcyclists this interaction may feel uneasy but bikers seldom even notice motorcyclists.

Civilians May Find MCs to Hang Around

For many potential Prospects it is during these brief interactions, where the MC mix with motorcyclists, that they find themselves drawn to the MC lifestyle and ultimately enlist into a mighty MC Nation.

Your Responsibility on The Set

As a Prospect it is important for you to know that your MC's reputation, ranking and status on The Set is determined by how the MC conducts itself while operating and handling its business on The Set. Your responsibility is simple:

- Bring no discredit upon your MC while you are on The Set! Your job:
    - Make sure that The Set is impressed by the conduct of your MC's Prospects (meaning: YOU) whenever you are on it.

Rules of Conduct on The Set

- On The Set, a Prospect is seen, not heard. In other words, keep your mouth shut! As a Prospect you should be observing and learning not talking and making mistakes that make your MC look bad. Be quiet and follow the lead of your full patched brothers. They will show you and tell you what to do.

- At no time should a Prospect be starting a fight on The Set. Trying to get 'street cred' and bolster a personal reputation could launch an entire MC Nation into a war that could cost your brother's their lives. Don't ever be the one to get some sh** started.

- Prospects don't chase women on The Set. Since you don't know all of the rules focus your prospectship on serving the MC while on The Set. Women who approach you are fair game. But you should always beware because chasing women causes more fights on The Set than any else.

- Whenever you are approached by a woman wearing another MC's colors never engage her without the permission of one of her brothers. When she approaches you and expresses an interest ask her which one of her brothers will give you permission to dance with and socialize with her. Accept no garbage from her like, "I do my own thing I don't need permission" because that may not be true. Insist upon knowing this information because it can be critical to your safety. Then ask your sponsor to take you to that MC's brother to secure permission to socialize with that woman in question.

- Treat all officers of other MCs with the same respect you treat your own MC officers. Acknowledge Presidents with respect and always address them by their title. Never interrupt two Presidents who are talking.

- Prospects do not have names on The Set. You will always identify yourself by your Prospect and number
  > "Good afternoon Prez I'm Prospect 9 of the Mighty Black Sabbath Motorcycle Club Nation Atlanta Chapter. It is a pleasure to meet you sir."

- Do not respond to people who ask you for your real name. They are only trying to get you in trouble with your MC. People on The Set know that Prospects don't have names. If you give someone your real name and you are prospecting for a traditional MC, you will get extra time added to your prospectship as punishment or pay a fine. Someone who is trying to call you by your real name on the Biker Set is attempting to disrespect your MC whether they know it or not (often women will feel sorry for you and say, "Don't call him Prospect, honey what's your real name?" Never fall for that!). The prospectship is to be respected. You will get a name at the end of the prospectship assigned to you by your MC. After you are blessed with a riding name (handle) you will be forever known as that name. Until then your name is Prospect X.

- Stay near your brothers while on The Set. You are a newbie and there are vicious people out there who want to start trouble. The closer you are to your brothers the better off you will be.

- Never talk negatively about ANY person or ANY MC while on The Set even if you are just talking to your brother or sponsor because you have absolutely no idea who may hear the negative things you may have to say. Even the walls have ears on The Set so you must always tread with caution. The civilian sitting at the bar having a drink while you are trashing the girlfriend of the Road Captain of another MC could be the brother of that Road Captain who just isn't wearing his colors that day. MC wars have started over less. Mind your mouth and keep it positive at all times.

- Never put your colors down on The Set. If you have to take them off for a second put them in a brother's hands and never on the floor, back of a chair or any other such nonsense. The reputation of your MC can suffer if you don't handle your colors properly. If you put your Prospect colors on the back of a chair for even a moment they will almost certainly be taken either by one of your full patched brothers, or worse, from the full patched brother of another MC. You don't want to be the one to have your colors delivered to your President by a full patched brother of another MC. It is best not to lose them in the first place. Keep them on your back. When you take pictures never wear your colors backwards. That is considered a sign of disrespect to your colors by many MCs. Take them off and turn them around and hold them instead.

- Watch, listen, look and learn everything you possibly can while you are prospecting on The Set. Be an observant "fly on the wall". Use this time to see everything you can and don't miss one thing going on before you.

- Take notes about things that may cause you to question. Then go over those notes with your sponsor and other full patched brothers. Keep a small pocket sized journal and jot down questions you have so that you can remember them to ask later.

No "I" in MC

There is no "I" in Motorcycle Club. That means that the interests of the individual drops and the interests of the MC becomes the most important aspect of your MC life from the time you begin prospecting until your MC career is over. For many of us, that day is when they close the casket and place us in our graves. The wise Prospect will always look to do what is best for the MC in every situation. If you begin thinking and acting in this way early on, you will never forsake the greater mission of the MC.

RESPECT

The defining glue that holds all of these disparate people together in peace can be summed up in one word: RESPECT! You will hear a lot about the Biker Set protocol wherever you go on The Set. Some protocol you will know and other protocol you will never have heard or seen before—especially as you travel to other areas. But if you show people respect no matter where you go or what you do you will be okay as you navigate the sometimes murky waters of the Biker Set and MCs. Treating people with great respect is better than knowing any protocol.

Protocol

I think of protocol as the eight letter word you always hear about when someone wants you to follow a certain set of rules they don't follow themselves. How does a Prospect learn the Biker Set protocol when different MCs, states, cities and locals have certain things they are more anal about than others? You will have to watch, look, listen and learn. Don't be afraid to ask too many questions to your sponsor. Take your cues from your full patched brothers. Apologize when you make a mistake and seldom make the same mistake twice. In time, your observations will pay off.

How to Learn Club History

You have to convince the senior guys to entrust you with their stories. You do this by being around when the full patched brothers want to talk. If you really want to know about the inner workings of your MC you have to know the stories the members have to tell. Get used to the idea that you will have to spend a lot of time around the clubhouse to truly get to know MC history. Think of your prospectship as an investment into the rest of your MC career. You also have to be good about not repeating the secret things MC brothers tell you. Be an open sponge that takes water in but let no water out—even if you get squeezed. Also read like a crazy man every printed thing you can find about your MC. Read the bulletin boards, old correspondence, web sites, posts on social media sites, anything you can find. The more you know the better off you will be.

How to Learn About the Members

Ask! Go up to your brothers during quiet times and simply ask them:

- "What would you want a prospective brother to know about you?"
- "What was your first bike?"
- "What do you love most about this MC?"
- "What do you hate most about this MC?"
- "What was your most exciting day as a member?"

- "What is the most important thing you want me to learn as a Prospect in your MC?"
- "What about your patch is most important to you and why do you see it as special?"
- "If something were to happen to you when we are riding together who would you want me to notify?"
- "What is brotherhood to you?"
- "What is your real name, first and last?"

Get the point? You can't learn about people if you don't take the time to get to know them. These folks will be your brothers and the women will be your sisters. Learn them well. Know them like an open book.

What if They Don't Like You?

Not every member will like you. Some will hate you. Some will hate you for no reason. Some won't know why they don't like you or distrust you—they just don't like you. Keep on plugging. Remove from them any reason to deny you your up vote. Always deliver what you promise on schedule or ahead of time. Be cheerful. Accomplish duties with a sense of urgency. Show up to be counted upon to handle the hard chores and mundane tasks. It will be difficult for a hateful member to continue to dislike you when you are handling MC business the way successful Prospects do. You may find some of them saying, "I don't really like him but damn he is a hard worker." At that point you have their earned respect. Being respected is worth far more than being liked!

John E. Bunch II 'Black Dragon' BSFFBS

Learn to Ride in the Pack

The MC is at its best on the road. After-all a MC is about biking, right? So what good does it do you to be afraid to ride two abreast and be absolutely useless when it comes to riding in the pack? Listen. A traditional 99%er law abiding MC rides two by two in formation. Get over it! You are going to have to drop your fear of riding two abreast and get with the program. Staggered riding is for those other MCs who wish they could look good in a pack. Practice makes perfect! So, practice, practice, practice, practice and practice!

Case Study 17: Riding in the Pack!

One technique I use to teach Prospects to ride two abreast is to ride into the increasing distal radial turns of my local mountain or canyon. I put Prospects in formation two-by-two and ride up and down that mountain or canyon ten or fifteen times. The whole time everyone is in formation never riding much faster than fifteen to twenty mph, riding the mountains slowly with your fellow Prospects or MC brothers next to you will teach you how to get to know the brother next to you so you can depend upon his riding skills and he can depend upon yours.

Get Help

If you feel uncomfortable riding in the pack, that is ok. Get a brother to take you out. Hang on the Road Captain's coat tails and tell him you need more instruction and confidence building. If you are prospecting for an elite, hard-riding motorcycle enthusiast MC then your brothers will be more than happy to invest the time into you to teach you how to ride safely in the pack.

Pack Signs & Road Signals

When the pack travels it uses hand signals to safely navigate from one destination to another. Lock steps with the Road Captain until you understand these signs and gestures and they become second nature. You should seek to become a competent pack rider so that any member will be comfortable riding side by side with you.

Bad Weather

Riding in bad weather can be challenging. You can easily get caught out in a rain storm, thunder storm, ice storm, hurricane, tornado, fog storm or lightning storm. As a biker you should routinely be familiar with the weather channels and at least check weekly for conditions that will be affecting your ride. Bring the appropriate clothing with you to confront all challenges. Put sweaters, rain coats, exposure suits, etc. in your saddlebags so that you will always have protection no matter what. Nothing can be more embarrassing than having to have a full patched brother hand you his coat or rain gear because the pack can't move forward because you are too cold to ride another mile. Plan ahead so that you can be the one passing out extra gloves and not the one always in need! Stay prepared! Look ahead! Keep up on the news! Have fun!

Cross Country Trip

Hard core riding MCs will give you big props for riding cross country as a Prospect. Some MCs may even require it, but not nearly so many these days as in times before. My advice is that every Prospect should take a cross country run if possible. If not, ride as far as you can in that Prospect patch on a trip with or without the MC.

Case Study 18: Riding Cross Country with Brother Bob

When I was a young Prospect I rode cross country with a man named Brother Bob (Robert Banks). Brother Bob took me in and taught me everything I needed to know about how to move my bike cross country. He taught me how to camp, live out on the open road, how to park my bike inside of the hotel room or put it on the porch and secure it so it could not be stolen while I slept. He taught me how to make time, make up time and make good time. He taught me how to ride across the hot desert and stay cool, how to maintenance my bike and how to ride in rain storms so bad you could not see ten feet ahead of you. He taught me how to pray and be thankful to God for my ride. He taught me how to ride next to outlaws, party with them and how to gain their utmost respect just for being a hard core rider. He was fifty and I was in my twenties. On his 50th birthday I was with him when his Gold Wing hit one hundred thousand miles. Now I teach Prospects what Brother Bob taught me. Thank you Brother Bob!

If you are a true rider, you will never be happier than when you are traveling across this country on two wheels and laying your head beneath the stars to sleep at night. Riding hard as a Prospect only sets you up to be even more of a beast on two as a full patched brother!

How to Make Yourself Valuable to the MC

- Always be the Prospect that can be counted on to get things done!
- Show up for every event while you are a Prospect. Miss none. Show up at every bike night, club run, activity and charity run. Become indispensable.
- Work yourself to the bone. In most MCs it is only a short time investment compared to the lifetime pay out!

Never Complain Except Through Your Sponsor

Your sponsor is the person through which you should voice your complaints and no others. Keep in good contact with your sponsor. Call him regularly. He is your liaison to the MC so communicate through him, complain through him, and work through him. Continually check with him to make sure you are progressing at an acceptable rate. If you are having troubles then it is your sponsor's job to fix those problems or present your problems to the MC. Your sponsor is your voice.

Overcoming a Terrible Sponsor

Sometimes you can just be assigned a terrible sponsor who never should have been anyone's sponsor. If this is your reality, overcoming your terrible sponsor will be key to realizing a successful prospectship. You can use the chain of command including going to the Sgt-at-Arms all the way up to the President if you feel you have a sponsor who is absolutely not handling his business. Be careful with that approach; however, because you don't want to be marked as a complainer or troublemaker. And you will still have to get that sponsor's vote to get into the MC. Most full patched brother's feel like a Prospect has no voice and therefore does not have the right to complain about anything. Another strategy is to identify a full patched brother who does seem to care about teaching you and latch onto him. Though not your sponsor he may train you, take up your cause, protect you and jump in your sponsor's ass to get him right. Careful navigation through these murky waters will require hard work, attention to detail, political savvy and a sterling reputation. A sterling reputation means that the full patched brothers know you to be a Prospect who handles his business and does more than is required at all times. Brothers don't mind helping out and going the extra mile for that kind of a Prospect. Gain that stellar reputation through hard work and by demonstrating genuine love and passion for the MC. Others will see you. Don't get the reputation of being a whiner!

Case Study 19: Overcoming a Lousy Sponsor

That reality happened to me when I was prospecting. My sponsor did not teach me and did not stand up for me when it was appropriate. He never taught me to ride in the pack, hand signals, maintenance, protocol or anything useful. He did; however, help me buy a car when my timing belt broke and for that I will forever be thankful, but as a MC sponsor he left a lot to be desired. I basically sucked it up and took it without much complaint. I observed others, learned a lot of lessons the hard way and eventually identified brothers who wanted to see me succeed and learned from them. The downside was it took me years to get into the MC. Don't let that be your reality!

The Loudness of Silence

There is a booming loudness in silence that you can use to your advantage. The quiet Prospect who speaks with his actions not with his mouth can learn by observation and listening where the loud mouth Prospect will only turn full patched brothers off! Let your hard work speak for you. Allow the brothers to hear your roar in your enthusiasm to volunteer and to handle the less glorious tasks. Let them speak to each other about how hard you ride—whenever they turn around they can see that you have pounded to another state or have escorted one of your traveling brothers to the state line or have ridden to the state line to escort your President home from a cross country trip. When they begin to whisper your name the volume becomes deafening and you have not even said one word. Be careful not to let it go to your head when they praise you. Be humble not cocky. Be bold through your actions not your arrogance. Be daring in accomplishing your goals and riding like no other Prospect has, not by bragging about what you have done after it is completed. Don't worry they will praise you should you deserve praise. Then take that praise, enjoy it and work to improve. Learn the loudness of silence and dare to excel!

Escorting the President

In many MCs, Prospects serve as security for the President while the MC is out on The Set. Remember that even though you may belong to a 99%er law abiding MC, this does not mean the MC does not have enemies or does not need to project strength and the ability to defend itself. 99%er MCs are not docile organizations that just lie down and take whatever may come—if necessary your brothers will overcome their enemies when pressed. Remember that when you wear a patch on your back you can expect that your MC will be tested from time to time. It is important that when the strength, will and determination of your MC is tested that the MC rises to the occasion. Freedom and liberty must sometimes be defended. The President is the highest ranking member of your MC. If you show him great respect so will others. If someone attacks or insults your President they attack the entire MC. When the President is on The Set a Prospect will always accompany him as a body guard. The MC will ensure their number one is protected. If this duty falls to you:

- Allow no harm come to your President on your watch.
- Stay focused while on duty, don't daydream or allow your mind to wander.
- Do not drink alcohol and lose your concentration while protecting the President.
- Do not chase women or gather their phone numbers while on watch.
- Do not allow others to walk straight up to the President. Intercept them and get the President's permission to allow them to get through your protection zone.
- Protect the President's drink if he should attempt to put it down, you take it, hold it and hand it back when he wants to drink some more of it.
- Never allow another MC to surround your President.
- Never allow your President to walk off on The Set alone.

- If your President is speaking to another MC President allow enough space for them to speak privately but not so much space that anyone can get to him.
- If your President is partying on The Set and having a blast and you are tired and want to go home—don't leave him, even if you have to go to work the next morning, even if he tells you to go on ahead without him. You will never be forgiven if you should leave the "P" and something happens to him when you should have been on watch. Suck it up! Stay on watch. Stay vigilant!

You Always Represent the MC

When you become a Prospect for a MC you no longer represent yourself. You now represent an entire MC Nation. You represent a brother who does not even know you exist in Inland Empire, California as much as you represent your local MC brothers whom you see every day in Jacksonville, Florida. Know that anything you do in those colors could cause the entire MC Nation to fall like a house of cards. You could get in an altercation and kill a man in Georgia which could cause your National President to go to prison in Canada. We are all tied together as ONE when we wear our MC colors. You could do something disrespectful to an OMC in New York that gets a brother beat down in Houston by the OMC brothers there. Don't screw around in our colors! We are 99%ers not hoodlums. Remember that when you want to run from the police with our colors on your back! While the news helicopter has our colors broadcast on national television, your National President will be on the phone with CNN explaining that we are not outlaws while live news cameras show you running from the police for the past hour! Do not break the law in our colors. Do not start wars with other MCs, beat your wife, sell dope, evade police, rob banks, or cause mayhem while wearing our colors on your back. Just a simple act like speeding through a town and cutting the Mayor's wife off then shooting her the middle finger can bring the entire police department down on our MC, all because of you! Your Prospect patch is not a license to become an emboldened bad ass. It is instead your license to demonstrate to all who see that we are a traditional 99%er law abiding MC Nation. Work to gain the trust of the community while wearing our colors. Believe me they are watching.

Women on The Set

The Biker Set has not been traditionally kind or fair to women. It is a male dominated arena where women seldom have dominant roles. Traditional 99%er law abiding MCs don't normally have women members. OMCs never have women members.

There are changes happening in the 99%er world where there are a lot of female MCs entering the Biker Set. There are also quite a few mixed MCs with men and women. But don't misunderstand women MCs have been around for quite some time. The Meter Maids MC is one of the oldest MCs in the United States—male or female.

For the most part women on The Set fall into these categories:

- –Civilians – Riders
- MC Riders
- Property

- Social Clubs
- Groupies
- Set Pass-Arounds
- Civilians – Non-Riders

Women Riders

These are independent women who ride bikes but don't wear colors. Beware some of these women ride harder, longer, stronger and ride more miles per year than any man around.

Case Study 20: Hard Core Female Biker

I am reminded of a lady biker I once met. She has more miles under her on a 600cc Ninja than almost any male rider I know. This woman must put 60,000 miles per year on two, bent over on a crotch rocket!!!! Don't think that women can't pound on two. You may be severely disappointed when she passes you up on the highway!

Case Study 21: "I'm Not Going to Race that Girl"

I was once approached by a woman bent over on a crotch rocket who wanted to race me. She just kept twisting her wrist and taunting, "Come on Prez! You ain't so tough. Let's get it on!" I said, "No way am I going to race you now be gone with you woman!" She asked, "Why not? You Scared!?" I said, "Heck yes, I'm scared. If I beat you everyone will call me a wimp because I beat a woman without mercy and if I lose to you everyone will call me that wimp who couldn't even beat a woman! This is a no win scenario! I'll just rather sit right here where I'm sitting! It is much safer that way!"

Women MC Riders

There are women who belong to female-only MCs and mixed MCs. Many are hard core riders as well. Always remember that women who wear colors must be approached according to protocol on The Set.

Property

OMC's women and some traditional 99%er MC's women are known to The Set as "Property" or "Property Of." Property enjoy a special protection from the MC as they belong either to the entire MC or individuals within the MC whose names will be on their backs under the word (i.e. "Property Of Wheatstraw"). Do not approach women who wear property patches. If they approach you find out whose permission in their MC you must have to talk, dance or spend time with them. Then go through your sponsor to get that permission. You can't date a property without her President's expressed permission. Many bikers have lost their lives messing with other MCs' property. Don't be that guy! There are just too many available women on The Set to lose your life over someone's property.

Social Clubs

SCs are organizations of women who wear colors and support the Biker Set. There are many SCs that are dedicated to The Set. Almost all SCs have charitable activities in their bylaws and they actually conduct all kinds of missions for charities. You can approach women in a SC but they will most likely dismiss you because you are a Prospect. Most women on The Set will never have anything to do with a Prospect. But then again, there are some who do. Your focus should be on the MC, however and working hard to become a member!

Groupies

Every group has groupies. Whether they are rock stars or astronauts, football players or bikers-- women like to be around strong, masculine groups of men who live life by their own rules. They hang around them in flocks we often call "groupies." To that end, bikers are the rock stars of the Biker Set and full patched brothers of a MC are at the top of the food chain. There are more than enough groupies to go around if you are into that sort of thing. Groupies are not necessarily familiar with The Set rules. They are civilians who dress up in leather on bike nights and try to score a biker. They may look like fish out of water but they can be complicated. Remember that it is hard to make a housewife out of a woman with the mindset of a groupie. Although I have seen it done on The Set I have seen things go south a whole lot more. Groupies are fair game for everyone to have sex with so do not lose your heart over a groupie. They are often very pretty but also very troubled. Tread lightly. If your sponsor says a woman is a groupie— she's most likely a groupie. Protect yourself accordingly.

Pass-arounds

Set pass-arounds are a step or two or three below groupies. Many are pros who are trying to score a buck or two. They find themselves passed around from one biker's bed to another's. Many have addiction problems or are runaways or a myriad of other bad things that go to make up a bad life that a bad girl is living. Avoid these women, Prospect! You really should not deal with a woman who has no respect for herself, other than to tell her that she is somebody and God loves her too.

Civilians

There are civilian women who know nothing about the MC or anyone around The Set. They will show up from time to time wearing something exquisite and looking like fish out of water. They are magnificent as well.

Pull Your Weight

When you are prospecting with a group of prospective brothers you must resist the temptation to let others pull your weight. Always pull your own weight! You will only regret it if your brothers figure you for a shirker.

Always be on Time

Don't misuse your prospective brothers' time. To be continually late is disrespectful. Manage your time appropriately. To love the MC is to respect it in all ways. Don't have the MC waiting around on you. Leave early to get there on time!

Know Your Place

The MC is a smooth operating machine that has checks and balances. Each contributor must know his place within the chain of command. If you wanted a loan for a car, would you ask the bank president for it? No. You would go to a loan officer. Prospects don't approach the Presidentof the MC to talk about matters that should be handled by the Sgt-at-Arms or the Road Captain. A Prospect should never attempt to interrupt a Vice President who is talking to a Business Manager. Know your place and stay in your lane. Act like a Prospect and contribute from your appropriate level. How can a Prospect attempt to give advice to a Road Captain? If you are asked for your two cents always give it respectfully—and then only to the point that it is necessary for your to contribute. Then quickly reassume your position and wait for the next time you may be asked to contribute.

The Colors

The primary visual identification of a member of a MC is the cut adorned with a MC-specific patch or patches, predominantly located in the middle of the back. In many 99%er MCs the patch is a one-piece patch that will contain the name of the MC and location most often including the city and state. 99%er law abiding MCs don't wear a state only bottom rocker patch. Now, I don't know of any case where a 99%er MC wears a state rocker but I don't know everything. There may be a case out there where this is true, but I've never seen it so I would not advise any new MC to try it. Outlaw MCs' vest back patch or patches contain the MC logo, the name of the MC, the letters MC, and a possible state, province, or other chapter identification. The vest and the patches themselves are collectively referred to as the *colors* or *cut,* a term taken from the early practice of cutting the collars and/or sleeves from a denim or leather jacket. [3]

There are many motorcycle riding clubs and other groups that wear patches on the back of their vests. Riding clubs won't have the letters MC on their vests although you may see a riding club with the letters MSP for Motor Sports Club.

The MC patches always remain property of the MC and not the member. Only members are allowed to wear the MC patches. Prospects' colors are a patch with only the MC logo affixed. Some MCs only allow the Prospect to wear a "P" or simply the name of the MC and the letter "P."

Admit When You Are Wrong

Prospect, no one is right all of the time. Don't be stubborn. You are well respected when you admit when you are wrong, take steps to correct your errors, apologize where it is appropriate, and then work to never make that mistake again.

If They Could Do It You Can Do It

Prospect, there will come a time when you are going to be overwhelmed, exhausted and indeed ready to walk away and quit. This is the time when you should become even more determined. Look around. Every full patched brother has been where you are today. Not one of those dog-eared bastards is any better than you. If they could do it you can do it! So now, get to it and do it!

You Are You

The colors don't make you a man. They don't make you bad or tough or even likeable. You are likeable, manly and important before you ever put our colors on your back. Bring what you have to offer to the MC. We will accept you for what you bring—good or bad. Do not live off of the greatness of others who have gone before you in the MC by thinking that you automatically transform the moment you put on our colors. Instead, contribute your all to the MC and remain humble. Then you will make the MC better because you now belong. And in building your legacy, brick-by-brick, you will make the MC great because you will become great!

Disloyalty

Disloyalty to the MC will never be tolerated. Traitors will always be dismissed. Keep MC business inside the MC. Never attempt to sleep with a prospective brother's woman. Never steal from the MC. Never lie on the MC. Do not tell your wife that you are MC business when you are cheating around. After she discovers your infidelity she will always hate the MC unnecessarily. Guard the reputation of the MC with everything that you are and in everything you do!

Conduct in the Pack

A Prospect never cuts up in the pack. A Prospect never breaks away from the pack. A Prospect never stunts in the pack. The safety of your brothers should always be your number one concern in the pack, not showing off! Causing the public to hate the pack because of poor conduct makes it tough on the MC to survive. Don't be that guy!

Law Enforcement Members of the MC

Prospect, just because you are a cop does not mean that you are exempt from obeying traffic laws while riding in our colors. It does not matter if you can flash your badge and get out of trouble when you are pulled over. When the public sees you misbehaving in our colors they won't be looking at the city's police uniform. They will be looking at you riding in our colors. You need to keep it legal too, officer Prospect!

Tell Them You Want In

When speaking with brothers as your prospectship is nearing its term and your vote is coming up make sure to let the brothers know that you want in. Tell them!

Stand for the Count

You have done all that you can do. You have given your all and loved the MC for all that you are worth. Now stand boldly with your chin up! You are worthy to stand for the count. Good luck!

I Did Not Make It

Don't worry. If you did not make it the first time up take the extra time the MC gave you to work on the areas where you are weak. Take heart. It took me nearly five years to cross over and I eventually became the National President!

I Did Make It

Congratulations! You did it! Now work on being the best member you can be. Go get that patch sewn on before they take it back. God bless you Full Patched Brother! You are now a member of a hard riding MC. Go show off that patch. Sleep in your cut the first night. You will sleep in it a lot. Beware the initiation will be tough!

Teach One

Go recruit a Prospect and teach him everything you know. You are now more than qualified to grow your MC.

Glossary

1%er: Initially a description falsely attributed to the AMA to describe some of the MCs that attended Rolling Gypsy race meets. It was alleged that the AMA stated that 99% of the people at their events were God fearing and family oriented. The other 1% were hoodlums, thugs and outlaws. Non-AMA sanctioned MCs thus being seen as outlaws adopted the 1%er moniker and embraced it as an identity. Over time the 1%er designation became exclusively associated with OMGs, criminal biker syndicates and some OMCs. Though not all 1%ers are criminals it is certain that the 1% diamond designation attracts law enforcement scrutiny like no other symbol on a biker's cut.

5%er: A member of a MRO. Only five percent of motorcyclists are involved with MROs that are dedicated to protecting the rights of the other ninety-five percent of bikers by spending money, dedicating time and championing pro-biker legislation.

80/20 Rule: A requirement held by some MC councils requiring all blessed MCs within a council's region to demonstrate, via a bike count that 80% of the MC's members have operational motorcycles at all times.

AMA: American Motorcyclist Association

ABATE: An organization started by Easy Rider Magazine to fight against discrimination toward motorcyclists, mostly helmet laws originally. Once called "A Brotherhood Against Totalitarian Enactments" or "American Bikers Against Totalitarian Enactments", ABATE now has many other names including "American Brotherhood (or Bikers) Aimed Toward Education". ABATE fights for biker rights and champions many issues well beyond helmet laws. Members often help charities. Membership comes with yearly dues and officers are elected from the active membership.

Ape Hangers: Tall handlebars that place a biker's hands at or above his shoulder height

Backyard: Where you ride often—never defecate there.

Baffle: Sound deadening material inside a muffler that quiets the exhaust noises.

Bike Count: To stem the tide of the so called "popup clubs" some councils require a minimum number of motorcycles to be in a MC before they will allow it to start up in their region. MC numbers are proven when the MC undergoes a bike count of its members; usually with all members present on their bikes.

Black Ball List: A list enacted by a MC coalition or council. It is directed at non-compliant MCs that serve to notify other MCs not to support the "black-balled" chapter nor allow it to participate in any coalition authorized Set functions.

Blockhead: The V-twin engine Harley, 1984 - 2000

Boneyard: Salvage yard for used bikes and parts

Brain Bucket: Small, beanie-style helmet (usually not Department of Transportation (DOT) approved).

Broad: A female entertainer for the MC. She may be a dancer or at times a prostitute.

Broken Wings: A patch meaning the rider has been in a crash.

Burnout: Spinning the rear wheel while holding the front brake. (Conducting burnouts while visiting another MC's clubhouse is disrespectful as it brings complaints from the neighborhood and invites unwanted police attention. Make trouble in your own neighborhood and be respectful with noise and other commotion while visiting others.)

Cage: Any vehicle of four or more wheels specifically not a motorcycle.

Cager: Driver of a cage. (Usually cagers are thought of as dangerous to bikers because they do not pay attention to the road.)

Chopper: A bike with the front end raked or extended out.

Chromeitis: A disease associated with a biker that can't seem to buy enough aftermarket accessories (especially chrome).

Church: Clubhouse ("Having church" or "going to church" is referred to as the club meeting at the clubhouse).

CLAP: Chrome, Leather, Accessories, Performance

Clone: A motorcycle built to resemble and function like a Harley-Davidson motorcycle without actually being a Harley-Davidson motorcycle.

Club Name: Also known as a "Handle". A name given to a MC member by his brothers most often based upon his character, routine, quirks and/or a noteworthy event that happened in the MC of which that member played a part. This is usually a name of honor and often indicates the personality one might expect when encountering that member (i.e., 'Bad Ass'). This name is generally accepted with great pride by the member and is a handle he will adopt for a lifetime. For instance, I once became annoyed with a member of the Black Sabbath Atlanta chapter for giving me a hard time when I needed him to break into my house and get the keys to my trailer so he could rescue me from the side of the road in Little Rock, AR nine hours away. He gave me so much grief about my trailer registration, working condition of my signal lights and notifying authorities before he would break in my place that I frustratingly named him "By-the-Book" instantly changing his name from "Glock." By-the-Book so loved his new name that when he later departed the Mighty Black Sabbath M.C. Nation he took his name with him and is still called By-the-Book to this very day. (It is an honor for the MC to name you and quite improper for you to name yourself!)

Club Hopping: The frowned upon practice of switching memberships from one MC to another. Traditional MCs have low tolerance for bikers who "club hop" as this phenomenon breaks down good order and discipline in MCs. In fact this was seldom done in the early days. Most coalitions and councils regulate club hopping and enact vigorous laws against it. Often OMCs refuse to allow former members to wear another MC's colors after serving in their OMC. A MC should generally ensure that a club hopper waits at least six months before allowing them to Prospect for their MC unless the former President sanctions the move.

Colors: Unique Motorcycle Club Back patch or patches

Crash Bar: Engine guard that protects the engine if the bike crashes

CreditGlide: A RUB's Motorcycle

Crotch Rocket / Rice Burner: A sport bike **Counter Steering:** Turning the bike's handlebars in one direction and having it go in the opposite direction. All bikers should learn this maneuver for safety.

Custom: A custom-built motorcycle

Cut: Vest containing the MC colors. The name comes from the practice of cutting the sleeves off of blue denim jackets.

DILLIGAF: "Do I Look Like I Give A Fuck"

DOT: Department of Transportation

Drag Bars: Low, flat, straight handlebars

Evo /Evolution®: Evolution engine (V-Twin, 1984 – 2000)

Fathead: Twin-Cam engine (V-Twin, 1999 – Present)

Fender / Fender Fluff: A female passenger who is not an Old Lady but simply a lady a biker has invited for a ride.

Flathead: The Flathead engine (V-Twin, 1929 – 1972)

Flash Patch: Generic patch sold at meets and bike shops.

Flip: Occurs when an OMC takes over a less powerful OMC or 99%er. This can occur against that MC's will and could be violent. The less powerful MC will flip from their colors to the dominant MC's colors.

Flying Low: Speeding

Forward Controls: Front pegs, shifter and rear brake control moved forward (often to the highway pegs).

Freedom Fighter: A MRO member dedicated to preserving or gaining biker's rights and freedoms.

FTA: "Fuck Them All"

FTW: "Fuck the World" or "Forever Two Wheels"

Get-Back-Whip: A two to three foot leather braid with an easy release hard metal clip that can be attached to the front break handle or the clutch handle. Often it contains a lead weight at the bottom of the braid with tassels that just barely drag the ground when the bike is standing still. This ornamental decoration can quickly be released to make a formidable weapon to be used to slap against offending cages that invade a biker's road space (to include breaking out the cager's windows). Either end can be used in an offensive or defensive situation. The Get-Back-Whip is illegal in some states.

Hard Tail: A motorcycle frame with no rear suspension.

Hang Around: The designation of a person who has indicated that he formally wants to get to know a MC so he can begin prospecting for them.

HOG: Harley Owners Group

Independent: A biker who is not a member of a MC, but is normally a well-known, accepted individual of local Biker Set (of a higher order than a hang-around).

Ink: Tattoo

Ink-Slinger: Tattoo Artist

KTRSD: "Keep the Rubber Side Down" Riding safely and keeping both tires on the road instead of up in the air—as in having a wreck.

Knuck/Knucklehead: The Knucklehead engine (V-Twin 1936 – 1947)

LE/LEO: Law Enforcement Officer/Official

Lick and Stick: A temporary pillion back seat placed on the fender through the use of suction cups.

MC: Motorcycle Club

MM: Motorcycle Ministry (Also known as 5%ers)

Moonlight Mile: A short adventure with a lady friend away from camp.

MRO: Motorcycle Rights Organization. These organizations seek to protect the rights and freedoms of bikers (i.e., ABATE BOLT, Motorcycle Riders Foundation, American Motorcycle Association, MAG, etc.)

MSF: Motorcycle Safety Foundation

OEM: Original Equipment Manufacturer

Old / Ole Lady: Girlfriend or wife of a biker, definitely off limts!

OMC: Outlaw Motorcycle Club

OMG: Outlaw Motorcycle Gang

On Ground: Refers to showing up on or riding a motorcycle instead of showing up in or driving a cage.

On Two: Refers to showing up on or riding a motorcycle instead of showing up in or driving a cage.

Pan/Pan Head: The Pan Head engine (V-Twin, 1948 – 1965)

Patch: The back patch is the colors of a MC.

Patch-Over: Like club flipping a patch-over occurs when a MC changes patches from one MC to another. This is acceptable and not looked upon unfavorably in most cases. 99%er MCs patch-over MCs they acquire because 99%ers don't enforce territory. This will be peaceful gentlemen's agreement that happens unremarkably and without incident. 1%ers flip MCs.

Pillion Pad: Passenger Seat

Pipes: Exhaust System

PRO: Public Relations Officer

Probate/Probie/Probationary: A member serving a period of probation until he is voted into full patched (full membership) status.

Probation: The period of time a Probie must serve before full membership is bestowed. This is the time distinguished from being a hang-around because the member is voted into the Probie status and is permitted to wear some form of the MCs colors. The Probie is also responsible to follow the MC's bylaws.

Prospect: A member serving a prospectship until he is voted into full patched (full membership) status.

Prospectship: The period of time a Prospect must serve before a vote for full membership is held. This is the time distinguished from being a hang-around because the prospective member is voted into the Prospect status and permitted to wear some form of the MCs colors. The Prospect is also responsible to follow the MC's bylaws.

Rags: Club colors or a Cut.

Rat Bike: A bike that has not been maintained or loved.

RC: Riding Club. A group that rides for enjoyment (perhaps under a patch) but members do not incur the responsibility of brotherhood to the level of a traditional MCs, modern MCs or OMCs. Members generally purchase their patches and don't often Prospect/Probie to become members. Rides and runs are generally voluntarily and there is no mandatory participation. RCs are still required to follow MC protocol when operating on the MC Set and would do well to know the MC laws and respect them so as not to wind up in any kinds of altercations.

Revolution™: The Revolution engine, Harley-Davidson's first water-cooled engine (V-Twin, 2002 – Present)

RICO Act: Racketeer Influenced and Corrupt Organizations. Initially, these laws were passed for law enforcement to combat organized crime such as the mafia. They were quickly used to prosecute OMGs, OMCs and some 99%er MCs.

Riding Bitch: Riding as the passenger on the back of a bike.

Road Name: Also known as a Handle. A name given to a MC member by his brothers and is most often based upon his character, routine, quirks or a noteworthy event that happened in the MC of which that member played a part. This is usually a name of great honor and often indicates the personality one might expect when encountering that member (i.e. Bad Ass). This name is generally accepted with great pride by the member and is a handle he will adopt for a lifetime.

Rocker: Bottom part of MC colors which usually designates geographic location or territory, though other information may be contained there such as the word "Nomad".

RUB: Rich Urban Biker

Rubber: Tire

Rubber Side Down: Riding safely and keeping both tires on the road instead of up in the air—as in having a wreck.

Run: Road trip "on two" with your brothers.

Running 66: Though rare it is sometimes necessary to ride without the MC's colors showing (also known as "riding incognito").

Shovel/Shovel Head: The Shovel Head engine (V-Twin, 1966 – 1984)

Shower Head: The new Harley-Davidson V-Rod motorcycle motor.

Sissy Bar Passenger Backrest

Slab: Interstate

Sled: Motorcycle

Softail®: A motorcycle frame whose suspension is hidden, making it resemble a hard tail.

SMRO: State Motorcycle Rights Organization. Same as a MRO except defined by the state in which they operate, (i.e., ABATE of Oklahoma, MAG of Georgia, etc.)

Straight Pipes: An exhaust system with no Baffles

Tats: Tattoos

Tail Gunner: The last rider in the pack

The Motorcyclist Memorial Wall: A biker's memorial wall located in Hopedale Ohio where the names of fallen riders are engraved for a nominal fee (www.motorcyclistmemorial.com). Memorial bricks may also be purchased to lie at the beautiful site.

The Motorcycle Memorial Foundation: The foundation that operates the Motorcyclist Memorial Wall. P.O. Box 2573 Wintersville, Ohio 43953. **Thirteen ("13") Diamond Patch:** This is a patch commonly worn by some Outlaw MC Nations. The "13" symbol can have several meanings referencing the thirteenth letter of the alphabet, "M", standing for Marijuana, Methamphetamines, Motorcycle, or the original Mother Chapter of a MC. In Hispanic gang culture, "13" can represent "La Eme" (Mexican Mafia).

Three-Piece Patch: Generally thought of as being OMC colors consisting of a top rocker (name of MC), middle insignia (MC's symbol) and bottom rocker (name of state or territory MC claims). Not only OMCs wear three piece patches but new 99%er MCs should stay away from this design and stick to a one-piece patch.

Turn your back: A show of ultimate disrespect is to turn your back on someone.

Twisties: Section of road with a lot of increasing, distal, radial turns.

Vested Pedestrian: Is a person who is in a MC and wearing colors, but does not own a motorcycle. Often thought of as a person who has never had a motorcycle, rather than someone who may be between bikes for a short period of time (i.e. a month or two).
Wannabe: Someone that tries to pretend to be a part of the biker lifestyle. (This is an excellent way to get your ass kicked!)
Wrench: Mechanic
XXF-FXX/XXFOREVER – FOREVERXX: Patch worn by MC members to represent their total commitment to the MC and every other member of that MC. XX stands for the name of the MC (i.e. Black Sabbath Forever Forever Black Sabbath).

Appendix A:
The Prospects' Proverbs

Daily Affirmations to Keep You Strong

Prospects Do Not Take Sides in Club Arguments

The wise Prospect does not engage in MC politics. Instead he stays quiet. He looks, listens and learns. He educates himself about the MC bylaws, history and member personalities. His time will come but he can never be voted into the MC if one side or the other is against him before he ever gets started.

What Am I Doing Right Now To Better Serve The MC!?

The wise Prospect asks of himself every day when he awakens, "What can I do today to serve my brothers and the MC better than I did yesterday?" Then he sets out to do those things.

Your brothers will know you are worthy of their name only through your hard work and service. Earn your way.

I Shall Not Pack While Prospecting

The Prospect's back seat belongs to the MC. They may need him to ride to the store or commit some other act of service for the MC. Therefore the wise Prospect will never put a woman on the back of his bike while in the company of his brothers or when he is going to the clubhouse. She may get in the way of his service to the MC. She will have to follow in the car.

I Shall Learn to Ride with the MC

A traditional 99%er law abiding MC looks best when it is on the road rumbling from point A to point B. What good is a prospect that becomes a member and is still afraid to ride two abreast in the pack? Therefore the wise Prospect practices riding two abreast until he has mastered the art of riding in the pack. He will use discipline to overcome his unreasonable fears and practice to overcome his practical fears from lack of riding skills.

I Shall Learn the History of the MC

I shall learn the history of my MC because riding without the knowledge of how my patch was forged is shameful.

Head Lights Do Not Point to a Clubhouse

The wise Prospect never parks his motorcycle pointing at the MC clubhouse. Always back your bike in, if possible. Pointing your headlights at a clubhouse for too long or parking with your bike pointing the clubhouse can be seen as very disrespectful.

I Shall Never Put My Helmet on the Bar

The wise Prospect never places his helmet on a MC clubhouse bar because if he does he will likely have to buy the whole clubhouse a drink.

I Shall Never Disrespect Any MC President or Other Officer

The wise Prospect affords the same level of respect to Presidents and officers of other MCs as he does his own.

I Shall be an Ambassador of My MC

The wise Prospect will tell himself, "It is my greatest hope that I bring nothing but honor and praises upon my MC. I shall conduct myself in my dealings upon the Biker Set, at all times, as an ambassador of my MC."

I Shall Surrender My Ego

The wise Prospect will tell himself, "I am determined to serve my MC with all that I am worth. My full patched brothers depend upon me. To my MC I will give my utmost!"

APPENDIX B: PROSPECT READINESS TEST

After spending several months prospecting many Prospects know absolutely nothing about the Biker Set and are as uninformed as full patched members as they were as Prospects. This test is by no means all inclusive but you can use it as a guide to begin your education:

1. In what city, state and year was your MC Nation founded?
2. In what neighborhood was your MC Nation founded?
3. How many members comprised the founding fathers of your MC Nation and local chapter?
4. What were the names and occupations of the founding fathers of your MC Nation?
5. What is the motto of your MC Nation and what does it mean?
6. How did your MC Nation obtain its first clubhouse?
7. What are the addresses of your MC Nation's mother chapter and your local chapters?
8. What is the birthday celebration of your MC Nation and all of your local chapters?
9. What is alarm code to get into the clubhouse?
10. What is mascot of your MC Nation?
11. What were the first motorcycles, makes and models, owned by the founding fathers of your MC Nation?

12. How did the founding fathers of your MC Nation learn to ride?

13. Describe your MC Nation's colors and explain the meanings, origins and symbols of all of the elements of the patch.

14. What was the name of the first brother killed on a motorcycle in your MC Nation; what year did he die and how was he killed?

15. Who are the racing heroes of your MC Nation? Why?

16. What is the history of the first MC split in your MC Nation and what happened to the members who split off?

17. What is the preferred bike color and style of your MC Nation?

18. How many years must you be in the MC before you are authorized to wear the MC's colors as a tattoo?

19. What is your MC's policy for the removal of their tattoo if you should leave your MC Nation?

20. How many years must you be in the MC before you are authorized to wear the MC's medallion or ring?

21. What are the bike nights of all your MC Nation's clubhouses?

22. What are the names of the Presidents of all of the chapters within your MC Nation?

23. When did the President of your local chapter join your MC Nation?

24. What are the telephone numbers and contact names for all of the chapters within your MC Nation?

25. How often are club meetings generally held throughout your MC Nation and when?

26. How many members are necessary to hold a quorum in your local MC?

27. What is the order procedure for how church is conducted in your MC Nation?

28. What are the monthly dues owed to the National Headquarters by all chapters in your MC Nation?

29. What are the real names, phone numbers, email addresses and emergency contact numbers for every member in your chapter?

30. What are the steps to becoming a Prospect in your MC?

31. Who can be a Prospect sponsor within your MC?

32. What are a sponsor's responsibilities?

33. When does a chapter President vote on a motion?

34. How long can your motorcycle be inoperable before you are required to buy a new one or turn in your colors?

35. What are the main responsibilities of the Road Captain?

36. Who are the Regional Presidents in your MC Nation?

37. How many miles one-way must a member ride to be recognized as a Nomad Rider in your MC Nation?

38. What are all of the award patches a rider can earn in your MC Nation?

39. If a MC member suspects that a brother is too drunk to ride what is their obligation to that drunken member according to your MC's bylaws or policies?

40. What is the MC's procedure for one member borrowing money from another member?

41. What is the procedure for solving a physical altercation between two members in your MC Nation?

42. What member of your MC is allowed to physically strike another other member?

43. What members in a local chapter can actually fine other members?
44. What members in your local chapter can actually fine the chapter President?
45. Under what specific circumstances may your colors be taken from you for an infraction against the bylaws?
46. If a local chapter president requests your colors what must be done before the president can keep your colors forever?
47. Who comprises your MC's governing Council?
48. Is your MC coed?
49. What can your wife or girlfriend wear to support the MC if she is not a member?
50. What is the status of women associated with your MC?
51. Does your MC have a First Lady and if so who is she?
52. What is the definition of a member in good standing?
53. What are the main responsibilities of a Prospect within your MC Nation?
54. What are the basic rules of conduct for a Prospect within your MC Nation?
55. Where are required patches to be worn on the vest of a Prospect and full patched brothers?
56. What is the quickest way to tell if you are dealing with a 1% outlaw MC Nation member if you greet him face to face and have not seen the back of his vest?
57. How can you distinguish outlaw colors from the back?
58. What is the definition of an Outlaw MC?
59. What is a 99%er MC?

60. What is a 1%er MC?
61. Is there a difference between an outlaw MC and a 1%er MC and if so what is that difference?
62. Where did the term 1%er come from?
63. What is the philosophical definition that sets 1% MCs apart from traditional MCs?
64. Who was the first person to lose his life in a clubhouse altercation within your MC Nation?
65. What criminal or civil actions, if any, have been brought against your local or national MC by city, local or national law enforcement agencies in an attempt to shut down, prosecute and/or fine your MC during its history and what were the outcomes of those charges?
66. What were the lessons learned from question 65?
67. What were the names of any members that have been murdered or accosted while representing your MC Nation?
68. What caused any second or subsequent MC splits within your MC Nation?
69. To whom do the colors, insignia, designs, patches, logos and other paraphernalia of your MC belong?
70. How many MCs has your MC Nation flipped or patched over and to what MC Nation did those chapters belong before they were flipped/patched over?
71. Does your MC Nation wears support patches for a 1%er MC Nation? If so, which one?
72. If your MC Nation wears support patches for a 1%er MC Nation, who are their enemies?
73. If your MC Nation wears support patches what areas of town, cities or states is it unsafe for you to ride in your colors without being in the company of your brothers?

74. Why is it important to always remember that you are representing every MC member within your Nation when you are operating out in public?

75. What is your MC's consequence to you if you rip your patch off of your vest?

76. What is the consequence for striking another brother of your MC?

77. What is the consequence for stealing from your MC?

78. What is the consequence for discussing MC business outside of the MC?

79. What is the consequence for posting MC business on social media?

80. What is the consequence for cyber-banging on social media?

81. What is the consequence for losing your colors?

82. What is the consequence for disrespecting your colors?

83. Should your colors ever touch the ground?

84. Should you ever let anyone outside of your MC hold your colors?

85. What is another term for the vest used to hold your colors?

86. What does the term backyard mean?

87. What is the 80/20 rule?

88. What is the AMA?

89. What is ABATE?

90. What is a boneyard?

91. What are broken wings?

92. Why is it against protocol to burnout in front of another MC's clubhouse?

93. What is a cage?

94. What is the rule about wearing your vest in a cage?

95. What does going to church mean in the MC world?

96.   What is the proper procedure for dating the property of a 1%er MC?

97.   What is the biggest no-no about parking in front of another MC's clubhouse?

98.   What happens if you put your helmet on the bar of a MC you are visiting?

99.   What does the term "Club Hopping" mean?

100.   If your President wants to Prospect a hang-around who was first a member of another MC what is the proper protocol to accomplish this?

101.   What is the proper protocol for approaching a girl with another MC's patch on her back to ask her to dance or go out?

102.   What is the proper protocol for passing an outlaw or senior MC on the open highway when your pack is traveling faster than theirs?

103.   What does counter steering mean and how is it done?

104.   To what does the term "Slow, Look, Lean and Roll" refer?

105.   What is the proper hand signal to flash to the pack when a cop/highway patrol vehicle is spotted?

106.   What is the proper hand signal flashed to the pack when debris is in the road on the left side of the bike?

107.   What is the proper foot signal flashed to the pack when debris is in the road on the right side of the bike?

108.   What is the proper hand signal flashed when the Road Captain wants the pack to assume a single file formation?

109.   What is the proper hand signal flashed when the Road Captain wants the pack to assume a staggered formation?

110. What is the proper hand signal flashed when the Road Captain wants the pack to assume the suicide (two abreast) formation?
111. When the Road Captain lifts his hand up to indicate a left or right turn what does the rest of the pack do?
112. What is the proper hand signal flashed when the Road Captain wants the pack to slow down?
113. What is the proper hand signal flashed when the Road Captain wants the pack to continue on while he drops out of the pack to view it for safety?
114. What is the proper hand signal flashed when the Road Captain wishes to change places with the Assistant Road Captain in the back of the pack?
115. What is the best way to cross railroad tracks in an intersection?
116. During a rain storm when is the road the slickest?
117. When braking a motorcycle what is meant by the term "reaction time?"
118. When traveling twenty mph how many feet does it take to bring a motorcycle to a complete stop including reaction time?
119. When traveling 80 mph how many feet does it take to bring a motorcycle to a complete stop including reaction time?
120. Why does the front brake have more braking power than the rear brake?
121. According to distribution of impact locations on motorcycle helmets during collisions studies conducted by Dietmar Otte, Medizinische hochschule Hannover, Abteilung Verkehrsunfallforschung in Germany where are most head injuries concentrated for motorcyclists?

122. What does DOT stand for and why is it important when purchasing a motorcycle helmet?
123. What is a flash patch?
124. What is a freedom fighter?
125. What does FTW mean?
126. What does KTRSD mean?
127. What does LE/LO mean?
128. What is an OMC?
129. What is an OMG?
130. Are cell phones allowed in your church meetings?
131. What is the consequence for secretly taping your church meetings?
132. What is an MRO?
133. What does the term "On Ground" mean?
134. What does the term "On Two" mean?
135. What does the term "Patch Over" mean?
136. What does the term "Flipping" mean?
137. What is a PRO?
138. What is a probie?
139. What are the major differences between an RC and a MC?
140. What is the RICO act?
141. What is a rocker?
142. What is a run?
143. What is a gypsy run?
144. What is special about a mandatory run?
145. What is a tail gunner?
146. What does the diamond "13" mean?
147. What is the significance of the three-piece patch?
148. What is the significance of turning your back on another MC or patched person?
149. What does BSFFBS mean?
150. What does DILLIGAF mean?
151. What is a 5%er?

152. What is a lick and stick?
153. What does the term "Running 66" mean?
154. What is a vested pedestrian?
155. What is a hang-around?
156. What is a civilian?
157. What is a "Property of"?
158. What is a House Mamma?
159. What is an ink slinger?
160. How often should the financial report be given at your MC's club meeting?
161. Where must your MC's colors be purchased?
162. What are your rights if you ever face your MC's disciplinary committee?
163. What is necessary for you to be found guilty of a charge in your MC?
164. Who are the closest MCs to your MC Nation who can be considered to love your MC like brothers and where your MC will always have a home away from home (allies)?
165. What is a dominate MC?
166. It is possible to Prospect for your MC without owning a motorcycle?
167. If you don't like the direction your MC pack is going you can simply leave the pack and take a shortcut and catch up to the pack later? Y/N
168. Folks can join your MC without prospecting? T/F
169. It is okay to pop a wheelie in the pack? T/F
170. It is okay to leave a brother in trouble? T/F
171. It is okay to screw a brother's old lady or wife? T/F
172. Can the Road Captain fine a member without a trial for infractions committed in the pack?
173. When can the Road Captain order a member not to ride their bike?

174. Does the Road Captain have the right to see a member's license, registration and insurance in your MC?
175. When is it okay to give out personal information about a MC member to someone outside of the MC?
176. It is okay for an MC President to attend a function thrown by your MC without being searched for a weapon if everyone else is being searched?
177. What is the ranking order for the way your MC rides in formation?
178. Where does a Prospect ride when escorting a senior member of the MC Nation?
179. What is the first responsibility a Prospect is assigned after he learns to ride in the pack?
180. What is 'packing' and is a Prospect ever allowed to pack?
181. Who was the first Godfather of your MC Nation and what was his contribution to the MC?
182. When did the original Godfather die?
183. Who is the Godfather of your MC Nation today?
184. When is the Road Captain considered the President of a local chapter?
185. What is required to take a leave of absence from your MC?
186. When are you allowed to retire from your MC?
187. Where are standard business cards ordered?
188. What is the email address of any MC member in the nation?
189. How do you get a MC email address?
190. What duties must a Prospect perform daily in your chapter?

191. Can a Prospect crossover without speaking with the National President, National VP or the High Council President in your MC Nation?
192. What is the name of the most honored veteran within your MC Nation?
193. When was the office of National President created within your MC Nation?
194. How many MCs operate in your town and what are the names of twenty-five of them?
195. What is the C.O.C.?
196. Who are the Banditos MC and where are they located?
197. What is meant by the term "Top 5" when talking about MCs?
198. How long have the Outlaws MC been in existence?
199. Who are the Hells Angels MC?
200. Who are the Black Pistons MC?
201. Who are the Mongols MC?
202. Who are the Sons of Silence MC?
203. Who are the Wheels of Soul MC?
204. Who are the Sin City Disciples MC?
205. Who are the Outcast MC?
206. Who are the Thunder Guards MC?
207. Who are the Hells Lovers MC?
208. Who are the Chosen Few MC?
209. Who are the Pagans MC?
210. Who are the Grim Reapers MC?
211. Who are the Hangmen MC?
212. Who are the Galloping Goose MC?
213. Who are the Highwaymen MC?
214. Who are the Warlocks MC?
215. Who are the Vagos MC?
216. Who are Sons of Satan MC?
217. Who are the Red Devils MC?

218. Who are the Sin City Disciples?
219. Who are Sons of Satan MC?
220. Who are the Peckerwoods MC?
221. Describe the colors of all the MCs mentioned above, when they began and where there mother chapters are located.
222. Name the OMCs in every state surrounding yours.
223. What is a supporter MC?
224. It is okay to walk into a MC representing your MC Nation without wearing your colors?
225. Should you have a Set of colors with you no matter where you travel?
226. What is the mission statement of your MC Nation?
227. Does handling a problem internally within the MC relive you of your legal responsibility to call law enforcement if you think a crime has been committed?
228. What are the rules for all members to stand duty at the clubhouse should your chapter have a clubhouse?
229. What are your MC's national and local website addresses?
230. Does your MC have a women's auxiliary?
231. Does your MC have a Support Crew?
232. What is the phone number and password used for your MC's conference calls?
233. How do you jump start a motorcycle?
234. When would you jump start a motorcycle?
235. Can you use a car to jump start a motorcycle safely?
236. How can one battery man on a motorcycle push another man on a motorcycle without a strap or rope or chain?

237. How do you pick up a heavy motorcycle like a Gold Wing or a Hog if it falls over and you are by yourself?

238. Does your MC ride in staggered or suicide formation?

239. Where is lane splitting legal in the United States?

240. When encountering a tornado on the open road should you take refuge under a bridge? Why or why not? (Refer to http://www.srh.noaa.gov/oun/?n=safety-overpass, especially slide 22 – this may save your life!)

241. What should be done to avoid tornadoes in open country?

242. If riding on the open highway and you encounter sudden heavy fog how should you seek to protect yourself?

243. When riding across country in extreme heat (100° F or higher) degrees what is one of your greatest mechanical concerns?

244. When riding across country in extreme heat (100° F or higher) degrees how can you quickly cool off if you feel overwhelmed by the heat?

245. When traveling cross country through various OMC territories what should your MC do before entering their territory?

246. If riding cross country what auto parts store will always carry motorcycle batteries?

247. How does the AAA 'club motorcycle towing package' differ from your motorcycle insurance coverage towing plan?

248. When riding with another MC where should your MC pack be located?

249. What is your local chapter's responsibility to your MC Nation?

250. If your MC chapter needs a bank account is it okay for a member to put that account in his name?
251. What is the purpose of the website www.praying24hours.com?
252. Why do you want to be a member of your MC Nation?
253. What do you bring to your MC Nation?
254. What do you want from your MC Nation?

APPENDIX C: THE MIGHTY BLACK SABBATH MOTORCYCLE CLUB NATION

The **Mighty Black Sabbath Motorcycle Club Nation** is a national, traditional 99%er law abiding motorcycle club whose members ride all makes of street legal motorcycles (cruisers at least 750cc and sport bikes at least 600cc). The Mighty Black Sabbath Motorcycle Club Nation does not belong to any governing organizations like the AMA but is law abiding and is not a 1%er Outlaw MC Nation. It is not listed by the United States Department of Justice or any other law enforcement organizations as an OMC or an OMG. The Black Sabbath MC derived its name from the actions of the Original Seven African American male founders who rode on Sundays after church. When the Original Seven were looking for a name to call themselves—they said, "We are seven black men who ride on the Sabbath day after worship, so let's call ourselves Black Sabbath!"

History

The Original Seven founding fathers of the Black Sabbath Motorcycle Club Nation taught themselves to ride on one Honda 305 Scrambler in the hills of a neighborhood called Mount Hope in San Diego, California in 1972. That bike, given to 'Pep', by a close friend was shared between them. The founding fathers mostly worked at the San Diego Gas and Electric Company or were enlisted in the US Navy. They practiced evenings and weekends on the Honda 305 Scrambler until they eventually learned how to ride and each bought a motorcycle. Afterward they gathered at each other's garages after church on Sundays to ride, tell tall tales and drink beers. By 1974, their wives united and revolted demanding that no more club meetings be held in their garages on Sundays because the neighbors kept complaining and the wives felt threatened by the strength of the brotherhood. Undaunted the founding fathers rented an abandoned bar at 4280 Market Street where they remained one of the most dominant, influential and successful MCs on the African American Biker Set since 1974 (over forty years at the time of this writing). The brothers got their colors blessed by the Chosen Few MC Nation and the Hells Angels MC Nation in February 1974 after getting their clubhouse.

Founding Fathers
The seven original founding fathers were:

- **First Rider:** Robert D. Hubbard 'Sir Hub' (SDG&E Electrician)
- **VP:** William Charles Sanders 'Couchie'(SDG&E Electrician)
- **Sgt-at-Arms** Alvin Ray 'Stretch'
- **Road Capt:** Paul Perry 'Pep' (SDG&E Meter Reader)
- **Asst Road:** Capt: Solomon 'Sol'
- **Secretary:** John Kearny 'Black'
- Unnamed brother whose name has been lost to us

Racing roots
The Black Sabbath MC was not complicated in its mission during the early years. It was comprised simply of seven men who loved to ride, mostly on Sundays, who were similarly possessed with an insatiable appetite for custom building "Choppers" and unbeatable drag race bikes. This is still true today. All bike styles are welcomed and racers are most cherished in the Mighty Black Sabbath Motorcycle Club Nation.

Battle cry "I came to race"
The MC's battle cry was fathered by Black Sabbath MC legend, fabled racer, Allen 'Sugar Man' Brooks, who once wrecked Pep's motorcycle (early 1970's) at the Salton Sea bike run/race event, without a helmet, at over one hundred ten mph. Pep warned Sugar Man that his bike was not operating properly and was excessively vibrating when it got to one hundred mph. Sugar Man told Pep to let him test it and Pep warned him not to go over one hundred mph. Of course Sugar Man exceeded one hundred mph and destroyed Pep's bike. After the accident Sugar Man was forbidden to compete as the MC deemed that he was too injured to race. The President

threatened to take his colors if he attempted to drag race the next day. Sugar Man said, "You can take these damned colors if you will. I came to race!" Sugar Man consequently won the drag racing competition despite his injuries thereby etching himself into the Black Sabbath MC's history books.

San Diego Mother Chapter

The Mighty Black Sabbath Motorcycle Club Nation's mother chapter clubhouse stood at 4280 Market Street on the corner for forty years. During most of that time the MC reined dominant as the most successful MC in San Diego and is the oldest surviving MC on the black Biker Set in San Diego. For decades the Black Sabbath MC clubhouse was the only clubhouse on the black Biker Set. During that time all San Diego and Los Angeles MCs came to San Diego to celebrate the Sabbath's yearly anniversary which was the first run of the year. Even to this day West Coast MCs gather in San Diego for the first run of the year established by the Black Sabbath MC.

Nationwide chapters

The Mighty Black Sabbath Motorcycle Club Nation has chapters across the United States from coast to coast but growth was initially slow as the MC never envisioned itself a national MC from its inception in San Diego in 1974. The Black Sabbath MC is the oldest surviving MC born in San Diego. The second charter was not given until 1989 some fifteen years after the MC started. Club racing legend Allen 'Sugar Man' Brooks took the colors to Wichita, Kansas where Knight Rider and Lady Magic, previously members of the Penguins MC, developed the chapter, subsequently becoming the oldest surviving MC on the black Biker Set in Wichita, KS.

In 1999, then National President, Pep, launched the Denver, Colorado chapter. Not long after, he assigned veteran member Leonard Mack to head up the Minneapolis, Minnesota chapter and two years later Dirty Red launched the St. Paul, Minnesota chapter. In 2004, Pep launched the Little Rock, Arkansas chapter with his nephew Lewis 'Doc' Perry who became the first East Coast Regional President. Two years later Doc launched the Oklahoma City, Oklahoma chapter with his high school buddy James 'JB' Baker as President. In 2008, National Ambassador and former mother chapter President Dewey 'Jazz' Johnson launched the Phoenix, Arizona chapter. By then the Wichita, Kansas chapter was all but dead.

Exponential growth was not seen until 2009 when then National Enforcer John E. 'Black Dragon' Bunch II convinced Sugar Man to come out of retirement and launch the Tulsa, Oklahoma chapter. Black Dragon reopened the Wichita, Kansas chapter using hard core recruiting efforts but could not sustain the re-launch until Lady Magic tapped her son 'Pull-it' and grandson Chris 'Chill' Hill to restart Wichita. Black Dragon simultaneously launched the Atlanta, Georgia chapter with former Oklahoma City member, Pappy, who had also grown up with Doc Perry. Later in 2009 Black Dragon launched the Houston, Texas chapter with Bernard 'Krow' Augustus who became the first Midwest/Central USA Regional President.

In 2010 the Atlanta, Georgia chapter was taken over by Black Dragon's former submarine shipmate, Leon 'Eight Ball' Richardson who also became the first East Coast Regional President. Black Dragon became National President in 2010 and patched over the Macon, Georgia chapter under Curtis 'Ride or Die' Hill became the third East Coast Regional President. Black Dragon then patched-over the Sic Wit' It MC in Rome, Georgia under President G Man.

Sugar Man's first cousin Jamel 'Huggy Bear' Brooks launched the San Antonio, Texas chapter by the end of 2010 and became the first West Coast Regional President when he assumed command of the Phoenix, Arizona chapter in late 2010. Huggy Bear patched over the Inland Empire, California chapter under the leadership of Big Dale in 2011. Big Dale eventually became the second West Coast Regional President. In 2012 National Vice President Tommy 'Hog Man' Lewis received a blessing from the Chosen Few MC to open the Las Vegas, Nevada chapter with then East Coast Regional President Huggy Bear. In 2012 the Jacksonville, Florida chapter was launched under President Prime. In 2014, West Coast Regional President Big Dale launched the Riverside, California chapter under President Bob O. At the time of this writing, there are seven more prospective Black Sabbath MC chapters seeking to gain entry. Hail to the forefathers of the Mighty Black Sabbath Motorcycle Club Nation! We hope they are proud of what their dreams have become. Amen.

Membership

A prospective member is allowed into the Black Sabbath Motorcycle Club as a "hang-around," indicating that the individual is invited to some MC events or to meet MC members at known gathering places. This period could last several months. It is the time for the hang-around to evaluate the MC as well as for the MC to evaluate the hang-around. If the hang-around is interested and the Black Sabbath Motorcycle Club likes the hang-around, he can request to be voted in as a Prospect. The hang-around must win a majority vote to be designated a Prospect. If he is successful he will be given a sponsor and his prospectship begins. The prospectship will be no less than ninety days but could last for years depending upon the attitude and resourcefulness of the Prospect. National President Black Dragon prospected for nearly five years before he was accepted. The Prospect will participate in some MC activities and serve the MC in whatever capacity the full patched brothers may deem appropriate. A Prospect will never be asked to commit any illegal act, any act against nature, or any physically humiliating or demeaning act. The Black Sabbath Motorcycle Club never hazes Prospects. A Prospect won't have voting privileges while he is evaluated for suitability as a full member but does pay MC dues. The last phase, and highest membership status, is "Full Membership" or "Full-Patch". The term "Full-Patch" refers to the complete one-piece patch. Prospects are allowed to wear only a small thirteen-inch patch with the letters of the local chapter (i.e. BSSD) and the black cross on it. To become a full patched brother the Prospect must be presented by his sponsor before the MC and win a 100% affirmative vote from the full patched brothers. Prior to votes being cast, a Prospect usually travels to every chapter in the sponsoring chapter's geographic region (state/province/territory) and introduces himself to every full patched brother. This process allows all regional chapter members to become familiar with the Prospect. Some form of formal induction follows, wherein the Prospect affirms his loyalty to the MC and its members. Often the Prospect's sponsor may require him to make a nomadic journey on his motorcycle before crossing over, sometimes as far as 1,000 miles that must be completed within twenty-four hours to ensure that the Prospect understands the Black Sabbath Motorcycle Club is a riding motorcycle club. The final logo patch is then awarded at his swearing in and initiation ceremony. The step of attaining full membership can be referred to as "being patched", "patching in" or "crossing over."

Command Structure

- National President
- National Vice President
- High Council President
- High Council
- National Business Manager
- National Ambassador
- Regional President
- President
- Vice President
- Sgt-at-Arms
- Road Captain
- Treasurer
- Secretary
- Business Manager
- Public Relations Officer
- Media/Web Design Officer
- Full Patch Member
- First Lady SOTC
- Full Patch SOTC
- Head Goddess
- Full Patch Goddess
- Support Crew
- Prospect
- SOTC Prospect
- Goddess Prospect
- Hang Around

- Special officers include Disaster Chief, Nomad, National Sgt-at-Arms, Enforcer, Support Crew Chief, Godfather and Godmother.

Colors

The Black Sabbath Motorcycle Club patch is called the "Turtle Shell". The colors are set out on a white background inside a black circle, inside a black crested shield, with the words Black Sabbath MC encircling the riding man. The crested shield on the sixteen-inch back patch gives the appearance of a turtle's shell when worn as it covers most members' entire back. The MC's colors are white, yellow, black and blue.

In the forty-plus year history of the MC the colors have remained untouched except for the addition of the shield in 1975 and the enlargement of the patch to sixteen-inch X forteeninch in 2009. The adherence to the original patch mirrors their adherence to the core values of the Original Seven founding forefathers.

Since the Black Sabbath Motorcycle Club does not claim territory like dominant 1%er MC Nations its members don't wear state bottom rockers. The cities of the chapters are named on the colors.

Racial Policies

Because the Black Sabbath Motorcycle Club was started by African Americans and its membership is primarily African American (90%) it is considered to be on the 'Black Biker Set" by biker clubs across America. However the Black Sabbath Motorcycle Club states that even though it was started by seven African American men who rode on Sundays, today it is a multi-racial organization that is accepting of all religions, with chapters across the United States from coast to coast. The Mighty Black Sabbath Motorcycle Club Nation is a brotherhood based on a unified lifestyle centered on riding motorcycles, living the biker lifestyle and embracing one another as extended family as close as any blood relatives.

Neutrality

The Mighty Black Sabbath Motorcycle Club Nation has followed all MC protocol in setting up its chapters nationwide. To that end it has received blessings to operate by dominants in every area in which it has chapters. As a neutral 99%er elite motorcycle enthusiast, riding MC the Mighty Black Sabbath Motorcycle Club Nation wears no support patches as it takes no political sides and does not align itself with OMC politics.

Women in the Black Sabbath MC Nation

A male dominated organization, the Mighty Black Sabbath Motorcycle Club Nation men belong to the brotherhood of the cross. Women fall into two unique categories—Women who do not ride motorcycles belong to the female support social club known as "Goddesses of the Mighty Black Sabbath Motorcycle Club Nation". Women who ride motorcycles belong to the "Sisters of the Cross MC of the Mighty Black Sabbath Motorcycle Club Nation".

Sisters of the Cross

The Sisters of the Cross MC of the Mighty Black Sabbath Motorcycle Club Nation (SOTC) is a female motorcycle club that rides under the full patched brothers of the Black Sabbath Motorcycle Club. The SOTC was established in 2011 by National President, Black Dragon. SOTC Prospects must be eighteen years old, own a motorcycle and have a motorcycle driver's license. The SOTC are called the "First

Ladies of the Black Sabbath Motorcycle Club" and the ranking SOTC is called First Lady. The SOTC MC was created to recognize the achievements of many of the Goddesses of the Black Sabbath Motorcycle Club who were buying, learning how to ride and getting licenses for motorcycles at an incredible rate. The Mighty Black Sabbath Motorcycle Club Nation sought to reward the hard work and passion to ride these women displayed by giving them their own MC under the auspices of the Mighty Black Sabbath Motorcycle Club Nation.

Goddesses of the Club
The Goddesses of the Mighty Black Sabbath Motorcycle Club Nation are the social club auxiliary that supports the MC. Goddess Prospects must be eighteen years old, be of exceptional character and devoted to serve the best interests of the Mighty Black Sabbath Motorcycle Club.

Mission Statement

"   1. To become the greatest riding motorcycle club in the world by pounding down great distances on two wheels, bonding on the highways and byways as family, camping out while riding to biker events or cross country, enjoying the wilderness, racing, competing, winning and experiencing our extended family by tenderly loving each other more and more each day!
2. To become the greatest motorcycle club family in the world by encouraging diversity within our MC, building strong, lasting friendships among members, instilling a sense of love, pride, and togetherness within our communities, by helping those in need through   "

volunteerism, by cultivating a mindset of moral, social responsibility amongst our members. And by inspiring our youth to achieve beyond all limitations which will leave a legacy of hope and boundless dreams for future generations of the Mighty Black Sabbath Motorcycle Club Nation to come.

National President

The office of the National Vice President was created by Tommy 'Hog Man' Lewis then President of the mother chapter and former mother chapter President Dewey 'Jazz' Johnson, in the summer of 2000. Paul 'Pep' Perry, the last original founding member left in the chapter, was elected the first National President. Curtis 'Mad Mitch' Mitchell was appointed first National Vice President one year later. Pep also created the office of National Ambassador to which he assigned Jazz. The National Vice President position was eventually terminated. In 2010, Godfather Washington of the Mighty Black Sabbath Motorcycle Club Nation died and Pep retired to become Godfather. National Enforcer and President of the Atlanta chapter, Black Dragon was summoned to the mother chapter in San Diego and was elected as the second National President of the Might Black Sabbath Motorcycle Club Nation during the February mother chapter annual dance. Black Dragon recreated the National Vice President office and recruited then retired former San Diego President Hog Man for the position. Black Dragon created the High Council President office to which he assigned Sabbath racing legend Sugar Man. He also created the High Council which consists of the President and Vice President of every chapter. Black Dragon also created the National Sgt-at-Arms, National Business Manager, Nomad, Disaster Chief, Support Chief and PRO offices.

Riding Awards and Designations

In order to challenge his MC members to ride harder and to distinguish the Mighty Black Sabbath Motorcycle Club Nation as a superior, elite motorcycle enthusiast riding MC, Black Dragon created the Nomad Rider program. In an article written in the Black Sabbath Magazine, Black Dragon stated, "A 99%er law abiding MC Nation is nothing if its members don't ride!" The Nomad Rider program recognizes and awards Black Sabbath Motorcycle Club nomad riders for their achievements. Some of the awards include:

- Nomad Rider = 1,000 miles one-way (N1)
- 1 K in 1 Day Nomad = 1,000 miles one-way ridden in twenty-four hours or less (N124)
- Nomad Traveler = 2,000 miles one-way (N2)
- Nomad Warrior = 3,000 miles one-way (N3)
- Nomad Adventurer = 4,000 miles one-way (N4)
- Nomad Wanderer = 5,000 miles one-way (N5)
- Snow Bear Disciple Nomad = one hundred miles traveled in sleet, snow or 18° F (SBN)
- Poseidon's Disciples Nomad = traveling through three states during continuous, driving rain (PSN)
- Great Plains Nomad = riding across the Oklahoma or Kansas great plains (GPN)
- Panhandle Nomad = riding across the great state of Texas (TPN)
- Great Winds Nomad = riding through fifty mph wind storm (GWN)
- 1,000 mile bull's horn = eleven inch bull's blowing horn, awarded to all Nomad Riders
- 2,000 mile Kudu's horn shofar = twenty three-inch Kudu antelope's blowing horn, awarded to all Nomad Travelers

- 3,000 mile Kudu's horn shofar = thirty three-inch Kudu or Blesbok antelope's blowing horn, awarded to all Nomad Warriors
- 4,000 mile horn shofar = forty-inch Kudu, Blesbok or Impala antelope's blowing horn, awarded to all Nomad Adventurers; can be Kudu, Blesbok or Impala.
- 5,000 mile horn shofar = fifty-inch antelope's blowing horn, awarded to all Nomad Wanderers; can be any horned cloven footed animal.

Violence

Violent incidents have occurred in and around nationwide clubhouses.

- In 2002, President 'Bull' of the Zodiacs MC was killed after he pulled a gun on his former Prospect who was partying at the mother chapter with a new MC in which he was interested. The former Prospect slashed Bull's throat with a knife when he looked away during the confrontation. This was the first killing ever committed at a Black Sabbath MC clubhouse and brought the city of San Diego down on top of the clubhouse. The City Attorney initiated a campaign to shut down the clubhouse, nearly finishing the Black Sabbath MC. The clubhouse was subsequently firebombed in retaliation for Bull's killing.
- In February 2010, the mother chapter at 4280 Market Street was again targeted by arsonists who attempted to burn it to the ground right before the 2010 annual. They were unsuccessful.
- In 2010, a man was fatally shot in a hail of gunfire outside the Phoenix chapter of the Black Sabbath MC clubhouse during an altercation over a woman. He died a block away while fleeing the scene. This incident caused the closing of the Phoenix chapter clubhouse.

- On 11 May 2012, San Diego mother chapter President 'Wild Dogg' was murdered in front of the Black Sabbath Motorcycle Club clubhouse at 4280 Market Street during a drive by assassination. The case is still unsolved and open.

John E. Bunch II 'Black Dragon' BSFFBS

EPILOGUE

"Everything that I stand so firmly against today, I once was! It is only through experience, pain, suffering and being blessed to learn life's lessons that I have evolved to whom I've become. "

John E. Bunch II

I was not a good Prospect. I was more concerned with myself than I was concerned about the greatness of the Mighty Black Sabbath Motorcycle Club Nation. I could have been better but I just did not want to do the menial tasks. I could never be counted on to lend a helping hand around the clubhouse or to do any of the dirty jobs. That attitude cost me the respect of the full patched brothers. It took me many years to win my patch. In some ways I was simply a sorry ass. No one then would have predicted I could ever become our National President.

I was hell on wheels when it came to riding across the country, showing the colors and representing the MC. Perhaps that was my saving grace. I out-rode the entire MC – no one rode farther or was in more places than I was and boy did I think I was somebody. I was arrogant and cocky when I should have been ashamed of my overall performance. It is possible to be great at one thing and terrible at another. I wish that I had focused on being a great Prospect all the way around. I decided that those who did not like me could just go to hell and it really didn't matter how they felt.

Twenty years later, when I became the National President, I had to face those brothers again—when many of them told me they would NEVER follow my leadership as I was not truly Black Sabbath. It took a long time to win their respect and backing. Wasted time that can never be reclaimed—it would have been better to do things right the first time. You see, I still had to win their respect even though for some it was more than twenty years later. The hard work it took to win them over as National President could have been done when I was a Prospect. You have a choice. You do not have to follow the path I chose.

Your MC career is the sum total of all of your efforts both good and bad. Start right!

Bibliography

AMA. *American Motorcyclist Association*. July 2012. 27 September 2012. <http://www.americanmotorcyclist.com/rights/motorcycleon lycheckpoints.aspx>.

American Motorcyclist Association History. *http://www.americanmotorcyclist.com/about/history*. 22 June 2014. Internet. 22 June 2014.

"The Real Wild Ones", Classi Bike Mark E. Gardiner. *ClassicBike.com "The Real Wild Ones"*. 1998. This article was written in 1998 and featured on Classic Bike website which is no longer available. 22 June 2014.

Wikipedia Battle Fatigue. *http://en.wikipedia.org/wiki/Battle_fatigue*. 22 June 2014. 22 June 2014.

WikiPedia Hollister Riot. *http://en.wikipedia.org/wiki/Hollister_riot*. 1947. Internet. 22 June 2014.

Wikipedia Outlaw Motorcycle Clubs. *http://en.wikipedia.org/wiki/Outlaw_Motorcycle_Gang*. n.d. 22 June 2014.

Wikipedia Post Traumatic Stress Disorder. *http://en.wikipedia.org/wiki/Posttraumatic_stress_disorder*. n.d. Internet. 22 June 2014.

Wikipedia Shell Shock. *http://en.wikipedia.org/wiki/Shell_shock*. n.d. Internet. 22 June 2014.

About the Author

John E. Bunch II 'Black Dragon' rode on the back of a Honda Trail 50 for the first time when he was six years old. Instantly he was hooked! His mother couldn't afford to buy him a motorcycle so he borrowed anyone's bike that would let him ride, on back roads and farms all over Oklahoma where he grew up. When he was 14 his mother bought him a Yamaha 125 Enduro. By the time he was seventeen his step father, J.W. Oliver, gave him a Honda CX500. He was known throughout the neighborhood as the kid who always rode wheelies with his sisters, Thea and Lori,

hanging off the back. He took his first road trip at seventeen riding from Oklahoma City to Wichita, Kansas to visit his Aunt Bernita and Uncle J.P. He knew then that he was born to distance ride! The nomadic call of the open road in the wind, rain, cold, heat—under the stars were home to him.

In the late 1980's, he found himself a young submarine sailor stationed in San Diego, California. He got into trouble on the base with a Senior Chief who gave him and his best friend an order they refused to follow. The white Senior Chief did not want to see the young black man's career ended over insubordination so he did Bunch an extreme favor and sent him and his friend, Keith Corley, to see black Senior Chief George G. Clark III instead of to a Courts Martial. Senior Chief Clark threatened Bunch and Corley with physical violence if they didn't obey the Senior Chief and worked out a solution that saved both of their careers. Later Clark invited them to 4280 Market Street when he discovered Bunch had a love of motorcycles. Bunch walked into the mother chapter of the Black Sabbath Motorcycle Club and was blown away to learn that the Senior Chief Clark was also known as 'Magic', former President of the Black Sabbath Motorcycle Club mother chapter. Bunch was consumed by the strength, unity and brotherhood he had never experienced before. He became a Prospect for the Black Sabbath Motorcycle Club. His insubordinate ways were not quite behind him, so it took Bunch several years to actually cross over as a full patched brother known as 'Black Dragon' in the Black Sabbath Motorcycle Club.

In 2000, Black Dragon began advising writer/filmmaker Reggie Rock Bythewood who co-wrote and directed the DreamWorks movie Biker Boyz. Black Dragon went to Hollywood and worked as a Technical Advisor on the film. Biker Boyz has often been credited with re-birthing the African American MC movement in the United States.

In 2009, Black Dragon brought the Black Sabbath Motorcycle Club to Atlanta, GA as President and an Original Seven founding member. He suffered his first setback in Atlanta during a coupe that cost him the Presidency of the Atlanta chapter in December 2010. In February 2010, he was elected to the office of National President and began his nationwide march to spread the Black Sabbath Motorcycle Club from coast to coast. By 2011, the Black Sabbath Motorcycle Club became the Mighty Black Sabbath Motorcycle Club Nation with chapters spread from the West coast to the East coast.

Black Dragon has published several biker magazines including: *Urban Biker Cycle News*, *Black Iron Motorcycle Magazine*, *Black Sabbath Motorcycle News Letter* and the popular blog www.BlackSabbathMagazine.com. In 2013, Black Dragon created the first MC phone app, *"Black Sabbath Motorcycle Club"*.

Today Black Dragon is building a Mighty MC Nation that rides cross country year round where no trailers are allowed! Black Dragon and Keith 'Alcatraz' Corley currently serve the Mighty Black Sabbath Motorcycle Club Nation as brothers of the Atlanta chapter.

Black Sabbath Forever Forever Black Sabbath
A Breed Apart
Since 1974

www.blacksabbathmc.com

www.blacksabbathmagazine.com

A Note from Black Dragon

Now what? You've read the book and you now know the power of the information held within. I want you to know that you can help other prospects navigate their way through the murky waters of the Biker Set.

If you were helped, educated or informed by this book there are a couple of simple things you can do to join me in remaking the MC world through knowledge, experience, education and love – starting with the prospects:

1. Buy this book for a prospect in your MC. If you believe Prospect's Bible can deliver good Prospects who become life-long, contributing members of your MC then I ask that you spread the word by buying them a copy.

    Give it as a gift or setup a reading group to discuss how Prospect's Bible applies to prospects in your MC. You can also write an honest review on social media, your blog, website, or on your favorite bookseller's website. There are countless ways you can help others by spreading this word. Prospect's Bible is not just a book worth reading, it's a vision and a plan worth following to get anyone started positively in their MC career thereby contributing a positive outcome to the entire MC community. It is a vision worth sharing.

2. Enrich other motorcycle clubs by buying this book for your brother and sister MCs on your set or those with whom you share alliances. Imagine if other prospects could have the benefit of the knowledge you've attained.

Thank you for your support! Send me a note anytime with questions, improvements, or your best prospecting tales. *JBII*

Made in the USA
Columbia, SC
04 May 2024